ASTROLOGY AND VIBRATIONAL

HEALING

By Donna Cunningham, MSW

Cassandra Press
San Rafael, CA. 94915

Cassandra Press
P.O. Box 868
San Rafael, CA. 94915

Printed in the United States of America

First printing 1988

ISBN 0-961587-58-x

Library of Congress Catalogue Card Number 88-71403

The use of the material described in this text is not meant to replace the services of a physician who should always be consulted for any condition requiring his or her aid.

Front cover art by Susan St Thomas. Copyright © 1988 Cassandra Press.

Other Books By Donna Cunningham:
An Astrological Guide to Self Awareness
Being A Lunar Type In A Solar World
Healing Pluto Problems
The Spiritual Dimensions of Healing Addictions
(with Andrew Ramer)
Further Dimensions of Healing Addictions
(with Andrew Ramer)
Mooon Signs: Key to Your Inner Life

This Book is dedicated to the
memory of my teacher, Richard Idemon,
in sorrow for all the books he never wrote.

TABLE OF CONTENTS

INTRODUCTION

As befits a book dealing with Saturn and beyond, this book has been seven years in gestation. I made a false start in the summer of 1980, transcribing lecture tapes and organizing some notes, only to drop it for work on *Being a Lunar Type in a Lunar World*. I continued to collect ideas, quotes, and printed material, and put them into file folders. I also continued to announce to the astrology community that I intended to write a book on the outer planets. They heard it so often, they began to lose faith, but I didn't. I knew the time wasn't right and didn't pressure myself to work on it. Early in 1983, I started again, making an outline, but started with the section on Pluto, and, Pluto, true to its nature, took control and became a book by itself, *Healing Pluto Problems*.

I also went through a profound disillusionment with astrology, because it doesn't go far enough. It uncovers problems extremely well, but presents no solutions. It is descriptive, not prescriptive. Once you see that a person has a difficult Mars, indicating a problem with anger, what do you do? Send him to therapy for a few years? Our clients don't have time for that…we as a race don't have time for that. We all need to get free of negativity as fast as we can in order to survive and have a better world.

To remedy this lack, I studied healing and changed from an astrologer whose whole life was astrology to a healer who happens to have astrology as a primary diagnostic tool. The reason for the delay in writing this book is clear now. I didn't want to give just another perspective on Saturn, Uranus, and Neptune. These planets are already beautifully conveyed by such fine astrologers as Doris Hebel, Steven Arroyo, and Liz Greene. I was waiting for the missing component which the healing tools supplied.

In the second book in this series, there are two chapters which will enhance your understanding of some of the material in this initial book: a chapter on the planets as essence, and a chapter on general observations about transits. The material about the essence of Neptune, Neptune transits, and healing tools for Neptunian quandaries appears in the second book, along with some special material for professional astrologers. Although this is a work on the outer planets, Pluto is not covered in either book, since it was thoroughly (one might say obsessively) covered in *Healing Pluto Problems*. That book might be considered Volume Three of this series.

In addition to the material on healing in both books, there are some exciting discoveries about the outer planets themselves that will be presented. They include the insights and healing potentials of the homeopathic approach to astrology and what I will be calling the Belt of Life Technique. The things I discover in working with the zodiac are not my discoveries but the zodiac discovering itself through me. The discoveries are there for anyone looking at life through the lens of astrology. Thus, I can say, with perfectly Uranian detachment, that there's a lot of wonderful material in this book. I'm not congratulating myself, but commenting on the wonder that is astrology.

An astrologer who discovers something new about the zodiac is not brilliant, any more than Columbus was brilliant for discovering America. America was there to be discovered by any sufficiently adventuresome soul, and as a matter of fact, it had been discovered before 1492. So, undoubtedly, has anything "new" about the ancient science of astrology been discovered before. What's exciting about astrology just now, however, is that there are so MANY Columbuses.

Unfortunately, we Columbuses get conceited about our own wisdom, when really it is the wisdom of the solar system, which we glimpse intermittently and which gets lost again when we fixate on some point of it as OUR system. Astrologers share the human trait of wanting to be RIGHT—in fact, we seem to have it in abundance. Being right is a concern of the planet Jupiter, and in one of French researcher Francoise Gauquelin's studies, she found that astrologers are characterized by a prominent Jupiter. (So are Nazis.) Once we get a system or a theory, we ignore all evidence which doesn't fit in and defend that theory at any cost Being Right all too often puts you in the position of being a jerk.

Even if you're not particularly concerned about Being Right, your economic survival as an astrologer, as well as your supply of status strokes, depends on Being Right. Nobody wants you to come and talk if you aren't convinced you're Right. Clients want you to be Right, too— that's what they're paying you for. Students are particularly greedy for you to be Right. So, even if you aren't Right, you quickly learn how to be.

The longer I study astrology—and, through astrology, people—the less I know for sure. As a second or third year astrologer, I KNEW a lot more than I do now...and was probably a jerk much more of the time. By the time I had been an astrologer five years, I was God's Gift to Astrology, already lecturing at conferences. Now, after 19 years in the field, I'm "famous" to the extent a serious astrologer can be, and more and more I find out how little I know. In fact, I'm finally on the verge of humility. Not there yet, mind you, but close. AND I'm fully conscious that my stance on not Being Right is just another way of Being Right. And so it goes.

V

LIST OF ASTROLOGY CHARTS

CHAPTER ONE

A HOMEOPATHIC APPROACH
TO ASTROLOGY

I was a social worker in hospitals and clinics for ten years before becoming a full time astrologer. Long exposure to traditional medicine was disillusioning, so I explored alternatives. One of the most intriguing was homeopathy, which is controversial in that it is extremely different from traditional medicine and not well researched. Whether or not it is a viable alternative to medicine, I feel the philosophy behind it can teach us a great deal. I was stimulated to apply these concepts to astrology and found they worked very well, particularly in understanding the psychological complexities of the outer planets and their transits. Furthermore, as we shall see, the concepts lead to logical healing approaches.

The Basic Concepts of Homeopathy

Breaking down the word HOMEOPATHY into two parts, you get HOMEO which means like or same, and PATHY, which means disease or illness. That in a nutshell is the theory of homeopathy—you cure an illness by using a substance similar to the disease in its effects. To stop a fever, for instance, the homeopathic practitioner would use a substance which would make a healthy person feverish, albeit in a much distilled form. The effect is to stimulate the body's defenses, as homeopaths believe firmly in the body's capacity to heal itself. To the homeopath, symptoms are not signs of illness but of returning health, resulting from the body's attempt to mobilize its healing forces and battle the disease.

In most cases, traditional (or ALLOPATHIC) medicine suppresses symptoms by using a substance which produces results opposite that of the disease. When symptoms are relieved but the underlying cause is not addressed, sooner or later a new problem emerges somewhere else in the body. The two places where allopathic medicine accepts the rule of like curing like are in vaccination, where a weak concentration of the disease is injected to stimulate the formation of antibodies, and in treating allergies, where repeated injections of the allergic substance are used to desensitize the person.

Another basic concept of homeopathy is that man is soul and mind as well as body. When all three are in order, the person is healthy, but when one of the three is in disorder, the person becomes sick. The person is sick long before the tissues become diseased, so it is superficial to treat only tissue changes, as traditional doctors do. Homeopaths further believe that we exist on four different planes at the same time: physical, mental, emotional, and spiritual. The closest traditional medicine comes to this wholeness is in psychosomatic medicine. Even there, the interaction of emotion and body is recognized, but the part played by spiritual factors is not. Many forms of alternate health care, such as homeopathy and chiropractics insist on a holistic approach.

One key concept of homeopathy is that of susceptibility. Viruses are around us all the time, and we frequently receive injuries, but mostly they pass by without doing any harm. We fall ill only when there's a disturbance on one of the four planes. During a flu epidemic, not everyone gets it, only those who are susceptible.

A related idea is that of individuality. The totality of each person, encompassing a history and status on all four planes, is completely individual, so the treatment, too, must be tailored to the individual. Two people may both have high blood pressure, but from different causes and requiring different treatment. In the visit to the homeopath, the totality of the person is examined and taken into account in the remedy. Homeopathy is far more complex than presented here, but these five ideas are the basis. Our next step is to take these ideas and apply them to astrology.

Like Cures Like

Since the principle that like cures like is the basis of homeopathy, it should also be the foundation of homeopathic astrology. Logically, if faced with a Saturn problem, we'd seek a Saturn remedy. I once saw a poster which claimed that work was a better cure for worry than whiskey was. Worry is a Saturnian trait, and hard work, involving self-disciplined progress toward a goal, is another Saturnian trait, relieving worry by doing something concrete. As the poster suggests, drinking to escape worry is no solution. That would be applying a Neptune remedy to a Saturn problem...an allopathic approach. The symptom is temporarily suppressed (you get high, forget your worries) only to have it reappear when you sober up.

We will use the concept of like curing like as a way of finding remedies for psychological complexes connected with the outer planets. It is one of the more useful applications of homeopathic astrology. To give an example, the chapter on fear shows not only where fear comes from but also how to overcome it. If fear of public speaking gets in the way of success (both Saturn-related difficulties), the remedy is also Saturnian—make a detailed plan of what you are going to say and practice, practice, practice.

We Can Heal Ourselves

The homeopath believes in the capacity of the body to heal itself, and that symptoms are signs of returning health as the body mobilizes its defenses. Applied to astrology, this says that people have the capacity to heal their problems, given the proper stimulation. As we create our own reality, we may provoke situations in order to heal ourselves. Many of the seemingly neurotic actions related to the outer planets are actually Inner Wisdom. For instance, where Uranus falls in the natal chart we often experience instability. Our selection of unstable people or situations may seem neurotic to the pop psychologist. Yet, Uranus is also independence, and by consistently choosing instability, we trick ourselves into greater and greater self-reliance. Crazy like a fox!

The idea that symptoms can be a sign of returning health also puts a different perspective on erratic behavior under outer planet transits. The symptom is part of the process of overcoming the problem, a way of mobilizing the defenses to meet a new demand. These defenses partake of the essence of the transiting planet. For example, a person having a Pluto transit may be withdrawn, avoiding former associates. The behavior may be alarming, considering we are brought up to believe there is something wrong with being alone. Time alone may be exactly what the person needs—time to think things through and decide how to change a painful life situation. Difficulties we draw to ourselves under transits may cause us to confront in extreme form the very problem we are trying to overcome—the ultimate abusive relationship, for example—so that we mobilize ourselves to change.

Transits often work by intensifying the energy of the planet—as though we had a double dose of Saturn or Neptune. Given this intensification, people may go overboard during a transit. This is particularly true with Uranus. People may have stifled their individuality for so long that when they finally decide to get free, they go a little wild. Conversely, those whose careers have been stagnating may get a Saturn transit and start working compulsively to make up for lost time. Similarly, if we've been suppressing a particular emotion and a Neptune transit puts us in touch with that feeling, it seems bigger than life. As we learn to cope, it becomes more manageable. My favorite of Jung's theories is the pendulum, which means that the further to one side we have swung, the further the pendulum has to swing in the opposite direction before we finally get balanced. We may go back and forth erratically at first (the transiting planet goes over the same spot several times), but we finally come to rest in a more balanced position.

In life, just as in medicine, we run the risk of suppressing symptoms rather than delving into underlying problems. You CAN get through a difficult transit with the emotional equivalent of pain killers. You can drink to escape worry—you can stay stoned for months on end, but it won't solve the problem and often, simply from neglect, it gets worse. At the very least, by running away from issues outer planets raise, you lose an opportunity for growth and insight that can result in better functioning.

The Four Planes and The Outer Planets

The third rule of homeopathy is that all four planes of existence—physical, mental, emotional, and spiritual—must be considered in diagnosis and treatment. What this contributes to astrology is a reminder of the many levels we operate on. Chart interpretation needs to be holistic, taking all levels into account before judging a particular aspect or transit.

For any external problem we have (finances, health, career, relationships), a metaphysically and psychologically sophisticated astrologer may be able to trace related mental, emotional, and spiritual difficulties, remembering that there may be a higher purpose behind any problem. To be holistic, the astrologer should recognize that the solution is a balance. When the concern is about a Venus problem (relationships), for example, the person must also meet Sun needs (self-expression), Saturn needs (accomplishment), and the needs of each other planet.

When we recall that symptoms are a sign of returning health, we need to broaden our view. What looks like a physical problem, for instance, may be the Higher Self's way of establishing a balance on the spiritual or emotional levels. Susceptible people with Capricorn rising, for example, might fall ill when transiting Neptune comes to their ascendant—only one of the possibilities under that aspect. The more positive potential would be psychic and spiritual awakening or creative development.

However, the seclusion and quiet reflection that accompanies illness can sometimes be the catalyst to bring the positive potential to the surface. If an illness did occur, its purpose could very well be to balance the scales. Capricorn rising people strive for self-sufficiency and hate to rely on others; while ill, they are forced to let their barriers down and allow others to help. Illness is often a brilliant move by the Higher Self, making people confront issues they wouldn't face any other way. In fact, Capricorn

Rising people are known for delicate health, perhaps for precisely the purpose just outlined, of balancing the scales. Naturally, the pattern of falling ill could be replaced with taking conscious responsibility for balance.

Susceptibility and Individuality

An important concept in homeopathy is susceptibility; only those who are susceptible because of a disturbance on one of the four planes will succumb to a particular disease. Carried over into astrology, this may explain why some people react badly to particular transits, while others having the same transit react positively or not at all. For instance, one person with Saturn crossing over the Sun reacts with depression, anxiety about encroaching age, and feelings of failure. Another suddenly blossoms into maturity, taking on new responsibilities, and setting a firm foundation for life. Both reactions are Saturnian, but the second embodies the positive expression, and the first embodies the negative. One is clearly more susceptible to the negative effects than the other.

The question of why susceptibility exists leads to the principle of individuality. Astrology's advantage is that the chart gives clues to individual susceptibilities, depending on the planet's strength natally and the history of recent transits by that planet. Those with a strong and rather difficult natal Neptune often try to escape from difficult feelings. They may bring unresolved feelings to the surface during a Neptune transit. Those with a less strong natal Neptune may have an easier time with Neptune transits, since not as much is repressed. Likewise, people with several planets in Cancer are more deeply affected by any transit to their Moon or anything happening with the transiting Moon—the full Moon or an eclipse.

Increased susceptibility may also come about when someone has recently had a number of transits by the same outer planet, especially to key points like the Sun, Moon, Midheaven, or Ascendant. Likewise, increased sensitivity may result from repeated recent transits to a particular point in the chart by first one then another of the outer planets. If Venus, for example, were transited by first Neptune and then Saturn, the person might come to feel very vulnerable in relationships. I call this getting SENSITIZED. In much the same way, repeated exposure to an outer planet at an early age can result in a life-long sensitivity. This would happen, for example, if Neptune was conjunct the Sun at the age of four and then squared the Moon at five. Thus, in judging susceptibility, it is useful to consider the person's history.

The Belt of Life Technique

Over the past few years, as a logical extension of homeopathic astrology, I have developed the Belt of Life technique. The name is a mild put-on, because the Greek word ZODIAC translates literally as Belt of Life. All Belt of Life really means is zodiac, but doesn't it sound grand? In fact, the zodia⌐ IS grand, and all of life is contained within it.

The wheel of the Zodiac is an inexhaustible source of insight into human nature and difficulties. Readers of my book, *Being A Lunar Type In A Solar World*, will remember the Cancer Rising wheel was used to explore Moon-related concerns such as premenstrual syndrome, obesity, and maternal burnout. We will use the method in this book, with different rising signs, to discover the nature of other problems. I believe you'll be astonished at how much light is shed. The problem always contains the seeds of the solution—in much the same way, horary astrology is based on the belief that the time of the question contains the answer.

For those who are not familiar with my technique, it consists of deciding which planet is most associated with a particular issue. Then set up a chart wheel and put the sign ruled by that planet on the first house. To understand adolescence, for example, this period of life has much in common with the planet Uranus, so you would use the Aquarius Rising wheel. Continue through the zodiac, placing the remaining eleven signs in sequence. Thus, with Aquarius Rising, Pisces goes on the second house, Aries on the third, Taurus on the fourth, and so on.

Each house represents a particular area of life, and the house/sign match-ups help us understand the true nature of the difficulty. For instance, Aries on the third house (communication) of the Aquarius Rising wheel shows the adolescent's tendency to be combative in speech, to tell it like it is. Scorpio falls on the tenth, the house which shows our relationship with authority figures, illustrating the teenager's tendency to resent authority, to react intensely to discipline, and to engage in power struggles.The entire wheel is explored in depth in the chapter called The Adolescent, the Perpetual Adolescent, and the 40 Year Old. Provocative insights are gained by using other wheels to explore various psychological difficulties throughout the book. The reader is invited to experiment with the technique to elucidate other areas of life.

It should be pointed out that the wheels are symbolic. That is to say, when we use the Capricorn Rising wheel to investigate depression, we are not talking about people who have Capricorn Rising, but about the phenomenon of depression. Yes, Capricorn Rising people do often have a depressive streak, so they might find the insights especially useful. But a great many others suffer from depression, and the wheel explains the state of mind and attitudes of depressed people, no matter what their rising sign.

Students of mine have experimented, placing their own natal planets within a given wheel (0 degrees of the sign as the cusp of each house) and found it useful. Nonetheless, I would recommend that you first read the wheels through to understand the basic nature of a given problem before personalizing it with your own chart. The profundity is in the sign/house combination rather than the fact that your own Venus or Sun falls into a given house.

Although the insights can be stunning, what is even more exciting is that the wheel contains not only the problem but the solution. That is the homeopathic application, where like cures like. Living out the negative expression of the sign/house combination creates the problem, while upleveling to the positive expression provides an answer. This was done in *Being A Lunar Type In A Solar World* to find solutions to Moon-related problems. The Cancer Rising wheel has Scorpio on the fifth house, which represents not only children but creativity and leisure activities. Scorpio's negative expression is resentment, while the positive is regeneration through solitude. In dealing with premenstrual tension, Scorpio on the fifth house showed how sometimes when you're in that state, you feel violent. The positive use of the combination is to arrange quiet, private time in that interval to pursue your own interests. In this book, we will again use the wheels homeopathically to search for answers to the problems we investigate.

We have begun to explore how these principles can be applied to astrology in a most enlightening way. Next, we will consider some ideas about transits, particularly how the homeopathic approach can lead to more productive use of the transiting planet's energies. Although this book is as much about the outer planets in the natal chart as in transit, a transit often motivates us to clear up difficulties in the natal chart.

A Homeopathic Approach to Transits

Since our theme has been to draw parallels between astrology and medical practice, it might be fun to follow a medical model in exploring the effects of outer planet transits. For each planet, we will consider, as doctors do, these four things: 1) symptoms, 2) relevant history, 3) diagnosis; and 4) treatment. (In medical jargon, this is abbreviated Sx, Hx, Dx, and Rx.)

Transits By Saturn

ON THE PHYSICAL/MATERIAL PLANES: When the health houses

of the chart—the first, sixth, and twelfth—are involved, Saturn transits could bring lowered resistance to disease, because under this influence people can become exhausted due to overwork or stress. Since Saturn's cycles are related to the process of aging, they suddenly become aware of the physical signs and tissue changes of aging, even though the process has gone on for some time. On the material level, bills and other obligations come due. People are required to work harder, take on more responsibility, and go back and rebuild things that weren't built properly in the first place.

ON THE MENTAL PLANE: People may be anxious about the future, berating themselves for their lack of accomplishment or for how short of perfection they fall. There may be pessimistic thoughts about their capabilities and potentials, compared with their ideals. Regardless of actual age, they are now obsessed with encroaching age and the desire to establish themselves more securely.

ON THE EMOTIONAL PLANE: Under Saturn transits, people may be swamped by depression, even to the point of melancholy, due to perfectionistic demands. These people are often overwhelmed by worry, anxiety, and insecurity. Fears of aging, failure, or poverty are common. There is often frustration and discouragement about their current lot in life and a yearning for accomplishment and recognition.

ON THE SPIRITUAL PLANE: Material desires and the drive for success may be so strong as to block these people from a sense of spiritual connectedness; or, conversely, people may be frustrated that responsibilities on the material plane keep them from their highest spiritual development. Insecurity about material goods and the demand for perfection may stem from an inability to trust in God to provide for us, and in the continuity of the soul past this particular lifetime.

HISTORY YOU WOULD WANT TO KNOW: Saturn has much to do with accomplishment, permanency, stability, and structure. You might want to inquire what life goals these people have set for themselves and where they feel they stand in meeting them. It is important to know how rooted they feel, and how well they deal with structure or with a lack of it.

Saturn's 28-year cycle is broken into critical stages every seven years, so ask how the people were feeling or what they were experiencing at ages 7, 14, 21, and especially 28, plus each additional 7-year period. You would want to know how these people dealt with Saturn's demands for increasing maturity and responsibility. In addition, look at recent important Saturn transits, such as Saturn to the Sun, Moon, Ascendant, or Midheaven, for sensitization.

In the birth chart, look for natal Saturn aspects to the Sun, Moon, Ascendant, and Midheaven, or a great number of Saturn aspects to know whether these people might be especially susceptible to Saturn transits. A strong tenth house or key planets in Capricorn would be another indication. Conversely, an individual with a comparatively unaspected Saturn might not have as much experience in dealing with Saturn's demands.

DIAGNOSIS: Saturn represents a continual process of growing and maturing in our ability to deal with responsibility, self-discipline, authority, and structure. It is the reality principle, wherein we are brought to terms with the demands of living on the material plane—which we chose, after all, for the progress we could make. The test is to keep balanced—dealing soundly with material goods and success without becoming entrapped by them; being responsible enough without taking away the responsibilities of others; learning to be self-disciplined without becoming so compulsive you forget to enjoy life; dealing with your own authority and that of others without becoming either too dominant or too submissive; and establishing structure and permanency without becoming rigid and inflexible.

We spoke earlier about the homeopathic view that symptoms are a sign of the entity's attempts to mobilize and fight stress. The symptoms often seen under Saturn transits—anxiety, depression, pessimism, and an upsurge of perfectionism—may be a sign that people are finally grappling with realities they've long tried to escape. They may be discouraged or self-condemning for a time, as they compare where they are to where they want to be; but if the transit is used as a jumping-off place for aiming at those goals, then the symptoms are a sign of returning health. (The chapter on depression explores this reaction and ways of counteracting it in more depth.)

TREATMENT: Fitting with the homeopathic rule of like curing like, it should be apparent that Saturn problems respond best to Saturn remedies. It should be a time for stock-taking and inventory, where people plan out goals and develop concrete steps to reach them. If there's a deficiency (for example, in education), this is the time to make realistic plans to remedy it. People who are worried about money should be making a budget, sticking to it, figuring out realistic economies, and saving money, even if it is only a dollar a week. Whatever your concern or wherever you may feel inadequate, Saturn transits are a time to bite the bullet, face up to reality, and take concrete, self-disciplined actions towards your goal. (More suggestions will be given in the section on healing Saturn problems.)

Transits By Uranus

PHYSICAL/MATERIAL: When the health houses of the chart—the first, sixth, and twelfth—are involved, Uranus transits may produce high blood pressure or some other circulatory problem, or people may become accident prone as they rebelliously ignore safety rules. (See the section on Uranus and Accidents for suggestions about prevention.) On the material plane, Uranus may signal lightning-like changes of an unexpected nature—Charlie Conservative gives up a secure, well-paying job and enters the counterculture; the seemingly perfect marriage collapses overnight; or the captain of the football team announces he's gay.

MENTAL: People begin to entertain startling new ideas—some politically radical, some socially unconventional, and some merely eccentric. A willful streak often enters into the thinking—no one else's opinion counts, for after all, they are years ahead of their time, and, oh so enlightened. These people generally recognize no authority but their own. They make sudden, earthshaking decisions.

EMOTIONAL: People are restless, excitable, and even explosive. Now that they've figured out what they want, they want it yesterday. Fairly often, they are in a willful, rebellious, and contrary mood...if the boss wants it one way, they are bound to do it the opposite way out of spite. The need to conform or to do what is expected by society or people in authority brings on a high degree of tension, which is often relieved by impulsive acts of rebellion.

SPIRITUAL: No traditional religion will contain them at this time. They strike out on their own individual and often eccentric paths. People under this influence are so convinced that they and they alone know the truth, that they begin seeking converts. If you don't agree with their enlightened ideas, you are an enemy or—worse—an ignoramus.

HISTORY: You'd want to examine how these people behaved under past Uranus transits, especially those to the Sun, Moon, Ascendant, and Midheaven. You particularly want to look back at critical Uranus transits over the last few years. Adolescence is a Uranian period, so you'd want to know whether that was stormy. Rebellious youths who settled into a conservative, conforming adulthood might be especially prone to earthshaking changes under major Uranus transits. In particular, the 38-40 year old period, when Uranus makes an opposition (180 degree angle) to Uranus' natal position, can often be a second adolescence, when many of the same issues are reactivated. These ages are considered in greater depth in the chapter called, "The Adolescent, the Perpetual Adolescent, and the 40-Year-Old."

In the birth chart, people with aspects between Uranus and the Sun, Moon, Ascendant, Midheaven, or a great many aspects to natal Uranus might be especially susceptible to Uranus transits. Similarly, crucial placements in Aquarius would increase suceptibility. Conversely, those with a weak or unaspected Uranus and nothing in the sign Aquarius might have a difficult time dealing with Uranus transits due to their unfamiliarity with nonconformity and expressing their individuality.

DIAGNOSIS: Uranus represents the process of individuation—that is, breaking away from the comforting but confining wombs of family, hometown, or conventional society and becoming who we fully are. It is the process of seeking our true selves, independent of what parents, friends, and society think we "ought" to be. Because the pressure to conform is so stifling, we suppress our true selves at a heavy cost to our well-being. The more startling and seemingly uncharacteristic the symptoms during a Uranus transit, the more suppressed the true self has been. Impulsive, rebellious behavior doesn't represent the true self, however, just the lengths to which people feel they have to go in order to establish their rights. We often go overboard at first in trying to establish new patterns, but ultimately settle into a milder and more comfortable sense of liberated selfhood.

TREATMENT: Under the rule of like cures like, Uranian upheavals in our lives can be made less shocking through Uranian support systems. For instance, Uranus rules astrology and a reading by a good astrologer can help us get more in touch with who we really are, free of society's definitions. Through astrology, we can anticipate Uranus transits and plan ahead for them, scheduling vacations or leaves of absence and saving money so we have freedom to explore new facets of ourselves. Freedom is likely to make agitation and rebellion less intense. Groups, organizations, and friendships are also Uranian, and we can consciously involve ourselves with people and groups who help develop the new parts of our identity. Often it is more comfortable and more intellectually stimulating to do this exploring with like-minded people.

Transits By Neptune

PHYSICAL/MATERIAL: When the health houses of the chart—the first, sixth, and twelfth—are involved, the person may be in a lethargic or debilitated state, prone to strange, nebulous complaints no physician can diagnose. The material plane? Immaterial, as far as the Neptune-influenced person is concerned. He's busy building castles in the air and then moving into them, lock, stock, and barrel. Perhaps it's just as well he's moving, though, because he hasn't paid the rent in months. He's far too spiritual for all that... or too much into his music, his art, his pint of booze, or his very own navel.

MENTAL/EMOTIONAL/SPIRITUAL: Try as I might, I cannot separate these three sets of symptoms when it comes to Neptunians...nor can they separate them for me! They're all the same...everything is everything...and it's really too bad they cannot communicate the wonderfully profound insights they're getting. In fact, at times they cannot communicate with you earth-bound mortals at all. They're in a fog, their thinking made subjective, emotional, and hazy. They are prone to being deceived by themselves and others, seeing what they want to see.

Emotionally, these are people with what seems to be a terminal case of the blahs. They're disillusioned with everything on the material plane, would get on an airplane and leave it all behind, if only they knew where they wanted to go or what they wanted to do. But since they don't know, there's nothing worth doing except to sit here and smoke another joint.

HISTORY: Neptune has to do with such diverse ways of transcending the self as schizophrenia, abusing alcohol, hard and soft drugs—on the negative side—and creativity, service to humanity, and dedication to spirituality—on the positive side. You might want to enquire gently (these Neptunians are hypersensitive!) whether the negative aspects of Neptune have been a problem, and if so, what means these people have used to overcome them. You would also want to find out their feelings toward the more positive sides of Neptune and the degree to which they have been willing to engage in them. To diagnose susceptibility, pay particular attention to recent transits by Neptune, and natal Neptune aspects to the Sun, Moon, Midheaven, or Ascendant. In addition, look to the birth chart for Neptune aspects to these four points to see if the person could be considered Neptunian. A strong twelfth house or key planets in Pisces would also make people Neptunian.

DIAGNOSIS: Neptune has an infinite quality—people grapple with their smallness and helplessness against eternity and the totality of the universe. Some do so by trying to blot it out—escaping from reality with or without chemicals to help. Some do it by identifying with others even more helpless, and helping them overcome their problems. Finally, some do it by joining with something greater than themselves—a cause or faith of some kind. On the whole, spiritual connectedness seems to be the healthiest way of dealing with this realization of our finiteness. It's necessary to achieve a balance between the material and spiritual worlds, as religious people can become unbalanced to the point of fanaticism. (I suspect, in fact, that any ISM is a Neptunian form of imbalance.) The chapter in the second book called When Does Psychic Become Psychiatric? considers this topic in greater depth.

Whatever course this struggle takes, it is an attempt to deal with our finiteness. We must only be concerned with whether the path helps people to achieve fulfillment and, ultimately, a better way of dealing with the real world. Symptoms of negative Neptune—escapism of any kind or heavy reliance on drugs or alcohol—are undoubtedly no more than mistaken ways of reaching through to the positive side of Neptune, which is spiritual connectedness with the All… with God and our fellow man.

TREATMENT: More in-depth suggestions will be given in each of the Neptune chapters in the second book. Nowhere has the rule of like curing like been so clearly demonstrated as with Neptune problems. The success of Alcoholics Anonymous and other such self-help groups is based on the principle of one alcoholic (one gambler, one drug addict, one whatever) listening to, identifying with, and helping another. The allopathic approach rarely works—when a non-alcoholic tries to help, alcoholics retreat into other Neptunian defenses, such as evasion, manipulation, deception, and seeming compliance which means nothing.

Another principle of Alcoholics Anonymous and its spinoffs is admission of total powerlessness over the addiction and willingness to surrender one's life and will totally to the care of God, as each understands him. As paradoxical as it seems, this admission of helplessness is the only way alcoholics can stop drinking. Yet this is like curing like…admitting total helplessness somehow mobilizes people's capacity to defend against that same helplessness. It's mysterious—but then almost anything about Neptune is!

Transits by Pluto

Since my book, *Healing Pluto Problems*, did not consider the homeopathic approach, I include this issue here.

PHYSICAL/MATERIAL: When the health houses—the first, sixth, and twelfth—are involved, it is possible for some severe illness to manifest, something which has been underlying but now becomes visible. Here, above all, remember that symptoms are an indication of returning health. If illness occurs, it's because we need healing and are going into a period where that is possible, if we reconstitute ourselves on the mental, emotional, and spiritual levels as well as on the physical. On the material and external levels, profound changes in goals, behavior, and orientation to life come about during a two-year period that may involve long periods of isolation.

MENTAL: People may be quite withdrawn, a state that may be alarming to outsiders. They may ruminate obsessively on the past, going over and over the same hurts and wrongs with great bitterness. The thinking can be quite paranoid at times. As time goes on, the obsessive thinking becomes more analytical and considerable insight can be gained, especially if there is exposure to therapy and psychological literature.

EMOTIONAL: Under Pluto transits, people dig into emotions about past experiences they may never have faced before, even going back to childhood. Bitterness and resentment are common feelings people may be dealing with. Emotions about past events can be intense, extreme, and very painful. While outsiders may see this emotional turmoil as symptomatic of illness, people going through it actually are healing themselves. The catharsis connected with the analytical insights gets polluted old emotions out of the way, so people can function on a healthier level.

SPIRITUAL: On the spiritual level, people often go through a death and rebirth. There may be great bitterness over some event (e.g. the loss of a loved one), leading to a crisis of faith—"If there were a God, He wouldn't let this happen." For people going through such a stage, God is dead. In all but the most profoundly atheistic, the God who is dead is the Old Testament God who dispenses guilt and retribution, particularly about sex. (The vengeful Old Testament Almighty is a peculiarly Pluto/Scorpio creation.) Once that punitive God is dead, people can be reborn in their spirituality, responsible for finding their own sense of right and wrong and a new relationship to God along with it.

HISTORY AND DIAGNOSIS: Look for the strength of natal Pluto and recent Pluto transits that would sensitize people to this one. Assess how capable these people are of analysis and introspection, versus how much blame for their difficulties they project onto others (the extent of their paranoia). If they generally exhibit negative Plutonian traits such as isolation, controlling self and others at all cost, and turning feelings back in on the self, these problems could come to a peak during a Pluto transit. You'd particularly want to know if these people were ever self-destructive (especially any history of suicide attempts), because self-hatred might intensify to a critical level during Pluto transits to key points of their chart. Given a history of this nature, you'd want to be certain they have had or are having successful therapeutic intervention.

TREATMENT: Specific healing suggestions for various kinds of Pluto problems are given in depth in my book, *Healing Pluto Problems*. However, some specific theraputic approaches are rebirthing, bereavement counseling, and primal therapy.

CHAPTER TWO

HEALING TOOLS AND THEIR ASTROLOGICAL CORRESPONDENCES

This chapter is not meant to be a complete course of instruction in the tools we will be discussing, but to introduce you to them and make you familiar enough with them to see how you could use them along with astrology. The beauty of these tools is that, unlike counseling, you can use them without having to go back to school for a degree. In fact, you can learn them fairly quickly and begin to test them in your work. Obviously, taking workshops, courses, or reading the books in the bibliography will deepen your understanding. It is recommended that you keep a special notebook in which you record what you did in various instances, why you chose that method, and what reactions or changes occurred. This will enhance your learning.

Please understand that I am not offering these tools as magical solutions to the problems corresponding to the outer planets. Such problems can be deep-seated, stubbornly resistant to change, and cause much suffering. You may have to persist with the healing tools for a considerable period of time and integrate them with other, more traditional disciplines, such as psychotherapy. But my experience is that they do produce far greater and deeper movement and change in these painful patterns than traditional therapy alone.

Color As a Healing Force

The art of color healing is an old one, which can be traced back to Egypt. The Hindus used it as part of their ayurvedic system of medicine. In England it is a well-recognized aid to physical healing. For instance, blue light has been useful in treating burns or inflammations, while red light has been used to vitalize depressed people or to help in weight reduction, as you can read in more detail in the books listed in the bibliography. Only in the United States does the powerful medical establishment insist on outlawing color healing, along with many other useful tools. Thus, if you actually set up an apparatus with colored lights or with plain light and gels of different colors from an art store, you could be in danger of prosecution; so I am not recommending that. No, gentle reader, the law must be upheld.

No one, however, has figured out a way to prosecute you for what you think. (Yet.) Or for what you wear. (Only for what you don't wear.) And healers, psychologists, and even industrialists are finding that the colors you wear or paint your walls have a powerful effect on you. For instance, it has been found that wearing blue can have a calming effect, while pink enhances cooperation and loving feelings. We will use the color blue in the chapter on Saturn and fear.

Much is heard in spiritual circles about light—surrounding yourself with white light for protection, seeing light around someone else, hoping someone will come to the light. It's as popular and almost as syrupy as talking about "vibes," but that's because vibes are real and so is light. Light is the most powerful healing tool available to us. If you are puzzled, I'm not talking about the kind of light you see, but the light in your aura, which has been recorded through Kirlian photography. This light is the source of the life force energy in everything, and, as physicists are discovering, is the most minute particle of the atom. The psychically awakened perceive this light around you in various colors which signify your emotional and physical state.

Not everyone can see the aura, yet everyone has one. So, too, do we all have the capacity to work with auric color. Working with white light is a familiar practice for many people who have been involved in meditations at workshops, conferences, or meditation groups. Apart from white light, which is good in all situations, there are meanings and purposes for each of the colors of auric light. Their meanings are more or less equivalent to the interpretations of auric colors you may have read in various books on psychic development and healing.

The Chakra System and Its Healing Potential

Another approach with implications for astrological healing work is the chakra system, in which blockages often correspond to difficulties with a particular planet. When you read occult and spiritual literature, you will often find reference to the energy body or aura. Visible within that body to the psychically attuned are centers or chakras, somewhat like energy organs, which regulate the flowing in and out of the life force. They appear as wheels or vortexes of spinning energy and color. Traumatic events or life situations can dam up this energy flow, creating blockages in the individual's relationship to the outside world. Rebalancing and energizing the chakras through techniques like those we will learn here is a simple form of healing with powerful results, something we can all do to help ourselves and others.

For instance, in the area of the actual physical heart is an energy organ called the heart chakra, which governs the flow of love energy, and which seems related to the planet Venus. When the heart chakra is blocked, overstressed, or damaged, relationship problems or a sense of lack of love can occur. Unless this vital center is restored, it is hard to transform the negative relationship patterns connected with Venus aspects to the outer planets.

Various theorists disagree on the subject of the chakras, both on the number of chakras and their placement or function. On some major ones, however, the agreement is stronger. Likewise, there is disagreement as to which planet belongs with which chakra. For instance, some say the Sun rules the heart center (after all, Leo and the Sun are connected, as are Leo and the heart), while others say it rules the solar plexus...solar referring to the Sun. In the various chapters, I will suggest that you work with the chakra or chakras whose function most closely approximates the aspect in question. For healing the difficulties connected with planets such as Saturn, it may be necessary to strengthen several of the chakras. Figure 1 shows some suggested connections between the chakras and the planets.

The first center, the root chakra, is located at the base of the spine. Blockages due to early or repeated uprootings or traumatic events in childhood could result in poor grounding and terror about survival. Difficult Moon, fourth house, first house or Saturn placements could prove damaging to this center. The second or sacral center has to do with reproduction and the flow of sexual energy; traumatic events could create either blockage or overemphasis of sexuality and in difficulties related to one's sex role or gender. Different locations are given for the sacral center, some placing it two inches below the navel, others saying that men have it in the area of the testicles. Negative sexual experiences or difficulty in childbirth might create stress to this center, as could difficulty in accepting the roles and stereotypes assigned by our culture to men and women. Clearly, this chakra might be related to the planet Pluto and to Mars.

The solar plexus area, just above the waist holds the third center. The solar plexus rules self-expression and self-concept. Blockages could lower self-esteem and self-confidence, or create its defensive opposite—egotism, narcissism, as self-centeredness. Difficult aspects to the Sun, especially by the outer planets, could create blockages in this area. We have already discussed the fourth or heart chakra, located in the area of the actual physical heart. Traumatic ruptures of relationships often leave heart wounds that, until mended, affect subsequent relationships and the ability to give and receive love from family, friends, and others. A badly wounded chakra can affect adjacent chakras, so, for instance, a heart center wound may also affect the self-esteem.

The fifth center, located in the throat, governs verbal or written expression and other forms of communication, as well as dealing with money. Obstructions get in the way of the free flow of self-expression and prosperity. The sixth or brow center, located between the eyes, has to do with mental clarity, creativity and psychic abilities. Obstructions to this center might result in mental confusion, obsessiveness, or psychic bombardment. The crown center is located at the top of the head and has to do with inspirational or meditative states, where one is in touch with the Divine; obstructions would result in feeling out of touch spiritually, losing that sense of connection with the universe, or erratic psychic and spiritual experiences and beliefs.

Figure 1: The Chakras and Some Planetary Correspondences

ROOT	CHAKRA	Moon and Saturn Problems
SACRAL	CHAKRA	Moon and Pluto
SOLAR	PLEXUS CHAKRA	Sun
HEART	CHAKRA	Venus
THROAT	CHAKRA	Mercury and Taurus
BROW	CHAKRA	Jupiter and Uranus
CROWN	CHAKRA	Neptune and Pluto

(Mars would relate to the energy body as a whole.)

The following exercise is a general cleansing for the chakras. It is not a good idea to work on one to the exclusion of the others, even when that particular one seems to be the core of your problem. Sometimes a chakra gets damaged when it is overused as a way of avoiding conflicts relating to neighboring centers. For example, the person with low self-esteem (the solar plexus) might try to resolve it by being sexually compulsive (the sacral or sexual center), using sexual conquests to bolster the ego. Ultimately, the sacral chakra could suffer secondary damage. The chakras are as intimately related as the organs of the body; stress to one eventually creates stress to all. Thus, it is good to do this general cleansing and energizing so that all are in balance before doing remedial work on a particular one.

Exercise One: The Fireball Clearing for Chakras

1) Using a particular meditative technique you may already know, go into

a deeper level of consciousness. Or, simply breathe deeply and count to three again and again.

2) Imagine that there is a protective bubble around you. Using your intuition, fill it with a particular color of light. White light is always a good choice, as it contains all the other colors. Remember the chakras and their location in your energy body.

3) Start at the root chakra, and imagine a fireball of light positioned at that location within the energy. Blaze up the fireball, so it consumes any dark areas in its path. Here obstructions would come from difficulty in getting grounded or from traumas related to parental love or to survival. As you move on to other centers, the ball will continue to spin as long as it needs to.

4) Move up to the sacral chakra and erect another fireball, which again blazes up and burns out obstacles. Here the intention would be to create a balanced and healthy outflowing of sexual, creative, and healing energy.

5) Move to the solar plexus and start a fireball there. In this area, the blaze would burn away barriers to healthy, balanced self-worth, including wounds to the self-esteem and feelings of inadequacy.

6) Move to the heart center and start a fireball there. The heart center, being so crucial and vulnerable, may need repeated cleansing, as deeper and deeper heart wounds surface. Here the fireball would burn away obstructions to loving and being loved.

7) Next, erect a fireball at the throat center, where it would burn away obstructions to communication and also to a free flow of money.

8) The brow center would be next, the blaze relieving barriers to the free flow of creative and psychic energy.

9) Finally, make a fireball at the crown, which would cleanse obstacles to meditation and inspiration.

10) Become aware intuitively of which centers still have fireballs spinning, in order to devote special work to them. Blaze up the flame brightly in those areas for a while before stopping them all and dissolving the protective bubble.

Repeat this exercise over a few days until the chakras seem clear. Later, repeat with colors given in various chapters of this book—for instance, with the blue for Saturn and fear. Let your intuition guide you. Repeat the cleansing periodically to avoid emotional and psychic overloads that can arise in daily living.

A Solar System of Healing Chants

The following system was channeled several years ago at my request by a very fine psychic named Andrew Ramer. These are apparently ancient chants for the planets, in which the sounds activate the part of our energy field or consciousness which each planet represents. They have a very strong healing effect, especially when done in a group. They act as balancers for a planet, so that, for example, either a very strong Mars (aggressiveness, irritability) or a very weak one (lack of assertiveness and initiative) can both be balanced by the Mars chant. Doing the entire set regularly as a meditation can serve to integrate and balance the energies of all the planets. The chants are reproduced on the facing page as Figure 2.

Figure 2:   The Planetary Chants

PLANET:	DO FOUR TIMES:	CLOSE WITH:
OPENING CHANT: Breath sound, wind, void		
SUN:	Oh Hay Yah	Oh
MERCURY:	Oh Hi Ti Nah	Ti Oh
VENUS:	Nah Ti Nah	Oh
EARTH/MOON:	Si Idriah	Neh Hah Mah Set
MARS:	Nayzi Day Hoh Hi Mah	Kah Kah
ASTEROIDS:	Si Ti Yah Kah	Mah Si Kah *
(Repeat asteriod chant until you feel done, then Ai Hey Poh)		
JUPITER:	Hi Su Mayo	Ay
SATURN:	Dah Ti Kah	Oh Ay
CHIRON:	Kah Si Mah	Kah
URANUS:	Nah Mitriah	Nah Simitri
NEPTUNE:	Oh Myss	Oh
PLUTO:	Ti Yah	Ah
CLOSING CHANT: Breath sound, wind, void		

* This chant refers to the asteroid belt as a whole, rather than to individual asteroids.[1]

In this system, your body is the Sun, the center of the solar system, and the planets are in orbit around it. Thus, Mercury is a tiny planet orbiting very close to your body, Venus is the distance of a hug away, the Earth and Moon (together in this heliocentric system) the distance of your outstretched palm, and so on all the way to Neptune and Pluto, which are so far away from you that they may be in the next room. Hold and visualize as much detail about the planets as you can as you go through the system. For instance, remember that Venus is torrid and humid, that Jupiter is the biggest planet in the solar system, and that Uranus rotates backwards to the rest of the planets. In the individual chapters, you will learn more about the specific chants and their uses. The chants are essentially phonetic and sound like they look, however a tape and booklet about them are available from RKM Publishing. The booklet also goes into much more detail about the system and its various healing uses.[2]

Planetary Rosaries

Is there a planetary energy you'd like to make more constructive use of? Is there an aspect in your chart that gives you a great deal of difficulty? One that you wish you didn't have? Is there a quintile whose genius has yet to manifest? You can make yourself a gift to strengthen or balance the energy of a planet or to heal the difficult effects of an aspect by bringing out the best of both planets so they can blend harmoniously.[3]

A nice gift to make for yourself might be a planetary rosary, a necklace or bracelet of beads representing one or two planets. Using the system of chants presented here, you chant with the beads. You can also wear it as a healing amulet. If rosaries or prayer beads hadn't satisfied some genuine need, they wouldn't have been "discovered" by so many religions throughout the world. Chanting a rosary is a soothing, meditative action, altering consciousness, and helping to restore balance.

The beads must be made of natural materials, such as wood, clay, glass, or stone, and the string must be organic material such as cotton, silk, or leather. If you have time to make your own beads, you can seal the healing vibrations into them even more powerfully by chanting the planetary chant aloud as you make them and, perhaps, by making them at an astrologically propitious time, as explained in the various chapters. You can make dough out of flour and water, color it with natural inks like beet juice, and bake them until hard. Don't worry about durability; you will not need to work with the rosary for an extended period. You might like to keep it for a refresher course, if you find yourself slipping back into the old pattern. You can also, however, make necklaces of more expensive stone, wood, or glass beads, wearing them continually as amulets for a while and chanting them when you remember.

The colors of beads you will be working with are not the traditional astrological colors for the planets, nor are they the same as used in the color healing sections of this book. What they seem to be are the colors for balancing those planets. The system seems to have internal consistency, so work with it.

SUN	bright red
MERCURY	purple
VENUS	bright green
MOON	white
MARS	black
ASTEROIDS	mottled
JUPITER	yellow
SATURN	brown
CHIRON	grey
URANUS	silver
NEPTUNE	mint or sea green
PLUTO	clear glass or light wood

Uranus, the planet of exceptions, is the one exception to the rule in that man-made materials are preferred, such as a glitzy, plastic mylar bead. Uranus, after all, rules science and synthetics. When you chant a Uranus bead, be conscious of its differentness. Let the fact that it is different stimulate your awareness that Uranus is always where we deviate from the norm.

If you are only going to use one planet's bead, perhaps because you wish to strengthen your expression of that planet, you would string the beads, chanting the main part of the chant for each bead, doing the closing syllables only when you have finished the whole rosary.

You may want to use beads for two planets which are in aspect in your chart, to channel their energies together more constructively or to heal a destructive pattern they represent. There is a particular form you would use to set up a healing rhythm. Use two beads of the innermost planet to one of the outermost. For example, if it were a Mars Saturn rosary, you would be working with black beads for Mars and brown ones for Saturn. It would be two Mars beads, one Saturn, two Mars, one Saturn, two Mars, one Saturn, until you reached a length you liked. (On the other hand, if it were a Mars Venus aspect, the pattern would be two Venus beads, one Mars, for here Venus is the innermost planet.)

The Mars Saturn chant would go: Nay zi Day Hoh Hi Mah, Nay Si Day Hoh Hi Mah, Da Ti Kah, over and over again. Even as you chant this to yourself, you can feel the stop/start quality of this aspect. As you chant a rosary over time, you learn a great deal about the ways the energies of the two planets work together, and you begin to experience how they can work harmoniously. It enhances the process to write out the keywords for both planets, ranging from the negative to the positive as we will learn in the various chapters, so that you can see the various ways they combine. For instance, a negative Mars Saturn use is constricted (Saturn) energy (Mars), while a positive one is responsible (Saturn) leadership (Mars).

You may find it pleasing and effective to put a larger or more elaborate bead of one of the two colors at the center of the rosary or in several places for a longer one. While you are chanting intently, it serves to center and condense the energy. Of the two colors, pick the one which pleases you most or which you most want to strengthen. If it is the innermost planet you have chosen, the larger bead can stand for two of the smaller ones, but chant on it twice. Put the proper number of the opposite bead on both sides of the large bead. (For example, if the Saturn bead is the large center one, you would have two Mars beads on either side of it, but if the Mars bead is in the center, you would have only one Saturn bead on each side, but you would chant twice on the Mars bead.)

Start putting the healing energies into the beads before you even make the necklace. Hold a handful of the beads and do the proper chant out loud for a minute or two. Keep the beads in separate containers. The more you handle the beads and chant them as you continue to make rosaries, the more the beads will take on the healing energies. (One reason for using natural materials is that they hold energy better.) As you string a particular rosary, imagine that you are drawing in energy from that planet's position in the sky. Chant the planet's chant aloud a few times with each bead, until you somehow feel the bead is ripe. String it and go on to the next, and the next, until the rosary is the length you want. Then tie it off and finish by chanting the entire string.

You can make the rosary more potent by making it at an astrologically propitious time, like when the Moon is traveling over one of the planets in question. The strongest time of all would be when those two planets are making an aspect in the sky. For the faster moving inner planets, this may happen quite regularly, and thus waiting may be feasible. For the slower moving planets, however, they may aspect one another only rarely and you could not wait. I did happen to make a particularly powerful Pluto Saturn rosary at the time they were conjunct in 1982, but this is a conjunction that only happens at 33 year intervals. (Other Pluto Saturn aspects happen every eight years.) You might also do it when one of the planets in the sky is making an aspect to the other in your chart. For example, if it is a Venus Saturn aspect you are working on, do it when transiting Venus is aspecting your Saturn or vice versa.

Chant the completed rosary all the way around, not more than once or twice a day for as many days or weeks as you feel the need. You will begin to be more aware of the way this aspect functions in your life. You may even be confronted with such situations more often and more consciously for a time, as your Higher Self provides you with opportunities to improve the combining of the two energies. The rosaries, like the chants, have a subtle balancing effect, bringing out the more positive effects of the planetary combination in the end.

When you are satisfied that the rosary has done its work, put it away. If you feel the pattern reasserting itself, do a refresher course with the rosary. You may also give it to someone else who has the same aspect. The more the rosary is used, and the more people who use it, the stronger it becomes. You CAN make a rosary for someone else, but only if you have those two planets in some kind of aspect in your own chart. Otherwise, simply give them the beads and instructions on how to do it.

The Flower Remedies

An important element was added to my healing work in the fall of 1981, when I was introduced to the homeopathic remedies of England's Dr. Edward Bach. These liquid formulas are designed to combat specific emotional and spiritual conditions such as fear, guilt, resentment, or a sense of inadequacy. Called the Bach flower remedies, they are derived from flowers, trees, and other plants, greatly distilled, like other homeopathic remedies are, past the level of chemical potency. Since they were developed in the 1930s, they have been clinically tested by the case method, with carefully recorded results. There is also one significant research study, which we will learn about presently.

The Bach remedies, 39 in all, are related to difficult emotional conditions and reflect the needs of the fearful era when they were developed. The world was in a great depression, and fascism was looming. Accordingly, there are a number of remedies for depression, with careful descriptions of the kinds of depression for which they are suited for. There are remedies for many other fixed emotional patterns which are difficult to eradicate by talk therapy alone. Flower remedies come in small stock bottles of concentrate, of which three drops are added to a one-ounce amber dropped bottle filled with spring water. A teaspoon of brandy or apple cider vinegar can be added to the diluted mixture as a preservative. Generally, the person takes four drops of the mixture four times a day, with rising and bedtime being excellent times.

For recovering alcoholics, use vinegar not brandy as a preservative. The concentrates themselves are preserved in brandy, so for alcoholics, I reduce the formula to one drop of each concentrate. This does not seem to bring up drink signals.

For the first few days, the remedies might produce an upsurge of the feelings they are designed to heal, in the kind of reaction we will be discussing later as a healing crisis. It's not that the problem is getting worse, you are just more conscious of it and of the thought patterns behind it. Increased consciousness, though uncomfortable, is part of the healing—ultimately, the thoughts sound so ridiculous and embarrassing that you become willing to change. As you keep taking the remedy, it evens out. You might need to take several bottles of the diluted mixture to change a long-ingrained habit, but the day comes when you realize you are different, that a situation that once would have made you fearful or depressed has come up and you didn't react in the old way.

I have used the remedies in my astrological and counseling work for the past several years and find them invaluable. The natal chart shows personality traits which get in the way of fulfillment, while the transits pinpoint which self-defeating traits are emphasized currently. Together, the natal chart and transits enable me to give remedies at the psychologically strongest time. It is frustrating for a client to gain so much self-awareness during a reading and then not have a direction to go in order to change.[4]

An extremely well-designed study to test the effectiveness of the Bach remedies was done by Dr. Michael Weisglas for his doctoral dissertation. He wished to test whether they were working only through the strength of belief, in a placebo effect. He first gave a series of psychological tests to three groups of people. One group was given an amber dropper bottle with nothing more than spring water and brandy—a placebo bottle. The second group was given an identical bottle with spring water, brandy, and four of the Bach concentrates. The third group was given the same setup with seven of the concentrates. Since the concentrates themselves are preserved in brandy, they all tasted and looked exactly alike. It was a double blind study; the people who distributed the bottles did not know if they contained the placebo or the real thing.[5]

The research subjects were retested on the same psychological examinations when they had been taking the remedies for three weeks and for six weeks. The tests showed that the group which had the placebo made no significant improvement, while the other two groups did show significant increases in self-awareness, self-confidence, well-being, vitality, and creativity. The group with seven concentrates in the bottle, however, did experience more stress and had more of a tendency to drop out of the study. This suggested to Dr. Weisglas that no more than three or four remedies can comfortably be given without cross-interference.

In addition to the Bach remedies, there are a large variety of other remedies developed over the past 15 years, including those made from gems in a similar manner to those made from plants. Just as the Bach kit reflects the Depression Era in which it was developed, the newer essences reflect the spirit of the humanistic 1970s, characterized by the Human Potential Movement and the growing openness to non-Western spiritual teachings. BLACKBERRY, for instance, is for conscious manifestation and creative thought, while MANZANITA is for groundedness, and SUNFLOWER is for harmonizing ego with the Higher Self. The special usefulness of this group of essences is in bringing the strengths of the individual to the fore, capitalizing on the positive, growth-oriented segments of the personality. The Bach remedies, by contrast, seem focused on eliminating the negative. Both are needed in emotional recovery, but it is as important to actualize the strengths and talents as it is to ameliorate the pain.

For more information about the remedies, consult the books listed in the bibliography, along with sources for ordering the remedies. In the remaining chapters and in the second book, we will discover which remedies are good for the various difficulties experienced with outer planet aspects, natally and by transit. An excellent tool for the astrologer, the remedies are easy to learn and enable you to give the client something more than insight. Knowing what transits are going on pinpoint crucial areas for the remedies to approach effectively, for transits motivate the client to work on a particular difficulty.

The Healing Crisis

Sometimes, as you honestly look at an area of your life you'd like to change, the problem seems to flare up. Things aren't really getting worse, you've just removed your blinders and discovered how bad things got while you ignored the problem. Your awareness has grown, not the problem. This flareup, which is called a healing crisis, happens with many efforts, from psychotherapy to the more esoteric. Some transits by themselves are a healing crisis, even if you make no special efforts to work through the issues they raise. Emotions you are suppressing may need to come out in order for you to resolve the difficulty, and so things may temporarily feel worse during the process. If you've been suppressing anger at a coworker's behavior for a long time, for example, a confrontation may be needed to clear the air and change the situation.

As I discussed in *Healing Pluto Problems*, this temporary intensification of the struggle feels almost as though the problem recognizes that its hold on you is being threatened, and therefore rises up as big and menacing as possible so you'll knuckle under again. The "IT" that is acting this way is not separate but part of your being organized to operate automatically. Under some earlier threat, this part served as a legitimate means of survival, but it persists and is inappropriately applied to new situations.

As an experiment, you might try communicating with your Neptune part or your Uranus part. For instance, you could sit down and write a letter which begins, "Dear Uranus," asking why you keep repeating a particular pattern in relationships with authority figures. Assume that the part is trying in some way to protect or help you, no matter how much the pattern hurts. An answer may come to you as you write, or it might come in some other form, such as a dream, but if you are genuinely willing to communicate with it, you will hear from it.

The healing crisis is important to keep in mind as you work with your own outer planet difficulties. The tools we will be using may well bring up unwelcome memories and emotions. For instance, in working with the exercises in the chapter on fear, you may become aware of exactly how much fear you do carry around. Fear may arise out of events which happened in your past, and you may try to attach them to something in the present, and because it's difficult to feel so much about things that happened so long ago. Don't try to rationalize the feelings away. Experiencing them and finding out where they come from is part of letting them go, and the end result is that you are no longer burdened. Avoid drinking, overeating, smoking too much, or using drugs or tranquilizers, for they will shut the process down or dull its impact. By neither acting on the emotions impulsively nor doing anything to shut them down, you get through them faster and have a better opportunity to heal yourself.

Is the healing crisis avoidable? Couldn't you just be healed in an instant? Probably not—your problems could drop away in an instant if you changed your consciousness, but outer planet problems are deeply entrenched, so you may not relinquish them easily. Most of us don't pull our hands away from the fire until it burns us. But you CAN choose not to beat your head against the wall.

Different Strokes

The idea of "different strokes for different folks" should be a cinch for an astrologer. Naturally, you don't use the same healing approach for a Uranian as you would for a Saturnian, and a Neptunian would be totally turned off by the things to which a Saturnian would respond to. In my book, *Healing Pluto Problems*, an entire chapter is devoted to exploring how the Plutonian responds to the astrological consultation and to healing efforts. While we cannot go into that kind of depth about Saturn, Uranus, and Neptune types in this book, here are some general principles.

In healing work, you might be prepared for the fact that a Saturnian is going to be tougher and more resistant to this kind of subtle influence. You may have to repeat the remedy for several months. Some people, like Neptunians and those whose transits have brought them to a point of readiness to be healed, can experience a strong effect immediately. The real hide-bound Saturnian needs a longer time. One factor is the crystallization principle which is so much a part of the negative Saturn spectrum, as well as the fear that change is going to destroy that laboriously built structure they hold so dear. Another factor is the pessimism, negativity, and caution of the Saturnian. If you can get them to do affirmations to offset the negative thinking, your healing work will progress much better. One positive thing about a Saturnian is that, if you can convince them that something will work for them, they will work hard and conscientiously at healing.

Uranians generally respond well to groups, especially the self-help variety where they can maintain their independence and not have anyone tell them what to do. Sometimes they respond best to the paradigmatic approach which, in plain English, is reverse psychology. ("What's the magic word to get an Aquarian to do anything you want? Don't!") You would want to appeal to the intellect and to curiosity, rather than to the emotions, even though the split with their emotions is one of the main things a Uranian may need to heal. If emotions are the problem, you'd have to hook them into being curious about what those split off emotions might be. You might also show them how society is programming them to ignore their feelings, so they might decide to defy society by feeling them. If you can make them think they thought of it themselves, so much the better.

Whenever their behavior is considered anti-social or "deviant," Uranians generally believe it's society's problem, not theirs, and that society needs to change, not them, so there's no point in your telling them they need to conform. Their mantra is, "F*** 'em if they cannot take a joke." They may listen to you better if you can outline social trends that pertain to their problem and even, if you can do it legitimately, show how they are ahead of their time. Involvement in social action is the best therapy of all for them, for after all, fixing society is one of the main reasons they incarnated.

As for the more esoteric kinds of healing taught in this book, give it a rest. You'll notice that the section on Uranus contains very little in the way of healing tools. They are likely to laugh you out of the consultation room if you suggest invisible light or the essence of flowers or chants from some spirit guide. Be prepared to cite your scientific evidence, and even then, the bottle of remedies you give them will probably grow green mold before they finally toss it out. Propose it to them as an interesting experiment in how it can work despite disbelief. Cite the way The Establishment has brutally tried to suppress these alternate healing methods. But above all, don't insist, or they'll be sure to rebel. Detach. After all, maybe they're right. Maybe it IS society's problem.

Neptunians, on the other hand, will swallow almost anything you tell them. Unless, of course, it contradicts what their spirit guide or their guru told them. Write instructions out clearly and in detail, for they easily forget or get confused by instructions. Your problem is to get them to do it on their own, for you may wind up being their next guru, receiving hysterical phone calls at all hours of the night. If some part of you is tempted to be the Rescuer, the Neptunian is tailor-made for you—a match made in heaven or hell. For that, you yourself may need to take what I call the Rescuer's Remedy—to distinguish it from Rescue Remedy. It's made up of the remedies RED CHESTNUT, for excessive maternal love, CENTAURY, for those who let themselves be taken advantage of, CHICORY, for those who want to make others over, and PINE, for excess guilt and blaming yourself for the mistakes of others.

Another part of the Neptunian character that you need to be aware of is the addictive side of their personality. If they are actively abusing some substance, whether it be alcohol, drugs, or even food, the work you do together will be affected, as such things block out the feelings and suppress the healing process. Ask very specific questions about their habits. If they say they don't drink that much, ask how many cocktails or beers a day, and whether it is more on the weekend. If they say they only use recreational drugs, find out how often they have to have recreation. Sometimes their idea of a good time is very different from yours and mine. Keep in mind, too, that Neptunians who are addictive personalities can lie very convincingly about their habits, mostly because they lie to themselves. Denial is a powerful defense in the development of addiction. You are better off not working with people who are actively addicted unless they agree to go to a program for their addiction, such as Alcoholics Anonymous or some treatment facility.

The Necessity for Responsible Use of These Healing Tools

Now that you have an overview of the tools we will be using, it would be important to caution you about their use. Each of these tools is powerful; several in combination are even more powerful. Thus it is important that you use them gently and cautiously, working slowly to test the sensitivity of the person to each tool. Some, for instance, are so keenly sensitive to the flower remedies that they get strong, immediate reactions and are quite prone to healing crises, while other people take a considerable length of time to have the smallest improvement. Colors can also catalyze strong reactions, and certain individuals will have difficult catharsis with some colors while other colors are perfectly comfortable. The reaction of each individual to each tool has to be monitored closely. This requires a willingness on your part to follow up on the reactions to and results of anything you recommend.

It also requires taking the whole person into account, and the astrological chart is an excellent tool for doing so. People with many difficult Saturn aspects, for instance, are in great need of clearing out fear, and yet may be expected to be keenly sensitive to the blue light and the flower remedies for fear. If a catharsis begins, they are likely to become extremely anxious about what is going on...being afraid of being afraid. Know who you are dealing with, and know what part of the chart is currently under stress due to transits. (To my way of thinking, healers, therapists, and health care workers who do not have astrology available are rather handicapped, but then what other point of view would you expect from an astrologer?)

Even having this degree and extent of knowledge about the person, one would still have to proceed with caution, as it goes without saying that casual prescription of healing tools is irresponsible. For instance, too many people with no formal background and experience in herbology, anatomy, chemistry, pathology—or even botany—are ready to tell you what herbs to use based on casual conversation with you...rather like the neighbor who gives you the pills her doctor gave her last year when she had some of the same symptoms you do. The same caution should apply to light, color, vibrational remedies, or any of the other tools discussed in this book.

Recommended Books About Healing

Books About Flower Remedies:

Bach, M.D., Edward, and F. J. Wheeler, M.D. *The Bach Flower Remedies*. New Canaan, CT: Keats Health Books, 1979. (Published in the UK by C.W. Daniel, Ltd., Saffron, Walden.)

The original descriptions of the remedies and their purposes by the man who developed them. Not as comprehensive or understandable as Chancellor's book, but considered the Bible on remedies.

Chancellor, Dr. Phillip M. *Handbook of the Bach Flower Remedies*. New

Canaan, CT: Keats Health Books, 1971. (Published in the UK by C.W. Daniel Ltd., Saffron, Walden.)

The best book about the Bach Flower Remedies. There are descriptions of each of the remedies with the purpose and personality traits it is designed to heal. There are case histories about each remedy, including the physical ailments of the person which cleared up as underlying emotional difficulties got better.

Damian, Peter. *The Twelve Healers of the Zodiac.* York Beach, ME: Samuel Weiser, Inc., 1986.

A treatment of the flower essences and their astrological correspondences. My only complaint about this book is that I didn't write it myself!

Gurudas. *Flower Essences and Vibrational Healing.* Albuquerque, N.M.: Brotherhood of Life, 1983.

A book on the various flower essences which has quite interesting things to say about correspondences between the forms of plants and their healing purposes.

Gurudas. *Gem Elixirs and Vibrational Healing. Vol.I and II.* San Rafael, CA: Cassandra Press,1985 and 1986.

A two-volume definitive work on the use of gem elixers, which are similar to flower essences in their derivation, but are based on healing stones.

Sources of Remedies, Books, and Supplies

BACH REMEDIES: Ellon Company, Box 320, Woodmere, N.Y., 11598 and Bach Centre, Mount Vernon, Sotwell, Oxon, U.K.

PEGASUS: Pegasus Products Inc., Box 228, Boulder, CO 80306 (800-527-6104).

Metaphysical Books

Bry, Adelaide. *Visualization: Directing The Movies of Your Mind.* New York: Barnes and Noble, 1979.

Well-written, simple book on how to create and use visualizations to achieve your goals.

Gawain, Shakti. *Creative Visualization*. Mill Valley, CA: Whatever Publishing, 1978.

One of the better how-to books on using visualizations and affirmations to help yourself.

Other Healing Topics

Clark, Linda. *The Ancient Art of Color Therapy*. New York: Pocket Books, 1975.

An excellent paperback on the healing art of color therapy as practiced in other countries. It focuses more on the physical and emotional effects of actual light and color, rather than the auric colors we are working with here; however the two methods can reinforce one another.

Wallace, Amy and Bill Henkin. *The Psychic Healing Book*. Berkeley, CA: Wingbow Press, 1981.

A simply written guidebook for psychic healing, espcially about grounding and shielding techniques. The best guide of its kind, very accessible. Sensible and down-to-earth.

1 Donna Cunningham and Andrew Ramer, *A Solar System of Healing Chants* Euclid, OH: RKM Publishing, 1982.
2 Order from RKM Publishing, Box 23042, Euclid, OH, 44123. $10.95 plus $1 postage and handling. You might also ask for a catalogue of their excellent tapes by many of the country's finest astrologers.
3 This section reprinted from Donna Cunningham and Andrew Ramer's booklet *A Solar System of Healing Chants*.
4 I have done a tape explaining the remedies and how to use them in astrological work with both the natal charts and transits. It is available from RKM Enterprises, Box 23042, Euclid, OH, 44123, for $7.95 plus $1 postage and handling.
5 Michael Weisglas, Ph.D., "Bach Flower Essence Research: A Scientific Study," *The Flower Essence Journal,* Vol..1:1 (1980), 11-14.

CHAPTER THREE

THE ESSENCE OF SATURN

Jupiter's good reputation in traditional astrology is surpassed only by Saturn's bad reputation. In my opinion, both need to be taken with a grain of salt. How can Saturn be so bad when it wears a halo? Actually, the development of positive Saturnian traits within our character allows us to accomplish something lasting in our lives—traits like self-discipline, perseverance, elimination of the frivolous, stability, and reliability.

The Saturn Spectrum

The essence of planets are neutral because there are various expressions of the planet's energy. Negative traits are just the positive ones carried to an extreme. Most of Saturn's traits, like most traits of all the planets, are positive until they're carried too far. The stability of Saturn is wonderful as long as it doesn't get too rigid. Ambitiousness about a goal is fine as long as you don't carry it to the point of ruthlessness. To be organized is a great thing, as long as you don't go to the extreme of compulsivity—making lists of your lists and getting anxious about not accomplishing everything on them, getting upset if somebody disturbs your schedule. Being responsible and conscientious is fine as long as you don't carry it to the extreme of being guilt-ridden. Realism and caution are okay as long as they're not carried to the extreme of being timid and pessimistic, afraid to try anything new. I characterize this dichotomy as Saturn Plus and Saturn Minus.

Saturn Plus Hardens Into Saturn Minus:

Perfectionism	becomes	Desire for Quality
High Standards	become	Unrealistic Demands
Structured	becomes	Rigid, Inflexible
Dutiful, Reliable	becomes	Guilt-Ridden

Cautious	becomes	Timid, Afraid
Realistic	becomes	Cynical, Pessimistic
Ambitious	becomes	Ruthless
Stable	becomes	Inert
Organized	becomes	Compulsive

Saturn comes in two varieties—reasonable and unreasonable. The unreasonable one is the rigid superego demanding perfection, an internal demon whipping and driving you on. It constantly compares you to other people and finds you lacking. People with Saturn aspects to the personal points (the Sun, Moon, Ascendant, or Midheaven) or with the personal points or several planets in Capricorn would be especially prone to this kind of unreasonable Saturn.

Reasonable Saturn, an ally in your drive for self-mastery and accomplishment, says, "I want to achieve this, so let me set about making plans on how to do it. Let me think how to make this goal a reality, how I can break it down into reasonable pieces so I can get to the top of the mountain. What do I need in my backpack and what can I leave behind?" When Saturn is used that way, it is a helpful influence. It is structure and self-discipline. Having standards and wanting excellence from yourself is fine; when you never let up, it becomes self-destructive.

Saturn and Rigidity

Saturn rules crystals and crystallization, structure condensing into form. In the human body, it rules the skeletal system and skin, and without it we'd be jellyfish. In our lives, it represents structure, which we need to some extent, but also our tendency to rigidify or crystallize into set patterns. Our defense mechanisms and ways of dealing with repeated situations tend to get rigid. When we cannot adapt, there's a dinosaur effect wherein we continue behaving in ways that once were successful but no longer meet today's needs. By Saturnian hard work, you may be successful, but if you're not flexible, given today's rapidly changing world, you won't continue to be a success. Actors who get typecast limit their success, and so do professionals and business people.

Saturn patterns are set early, certainly by the first Saturn square to its natal position, at age seven. Childhood coping mechanisms needed to succeed in the family may not serve you out in the real world. For instance, as we will see later, people with Venus Saturn aspects had to act a certain way to get their parents to love them, but these behaviors don't necessarily bring them love in the outside world.

Those with Saturn aspects to the personal points (the Sun, Moon,

Ascendant, or Midheaven) have often had to be very Saturnian at an early age, that is, very serious and responsible. Such people tend to get crystallized too early, and at an immature level. Saturn's cycles represent the process of maturation, and yet paradoxically, our Saturn positions can show the place we are most immature—where maturity got sacrificed in the name of duty. No child of seven can successfully be an adult, so seven-year-olds who have to take on adult responsibilities tend to freeze at that level in important developmental tasks, such as social skills. Where Saturn is, the shell of adulthood may be present, but underneath is a frightened child, feeling overwhelmed and inadequate to meet these impossible demands. Even into adulthood, we may stay frozen there, as we are so fearful of failure that we put up rigid defenses which keep us from growing.

The degree of natal Saturn gives clues as to when this crystallization may have occurred, while the house, sign, and hard aspects to other planets can show the exact area of life it occurred in and why. A man with Saturn at 16 degrees of Scorpio in the tenth house had to take on a large degree of responsibility when he was 16 because his father died of alcoholism. There was much resentment of this burden, which included having to get a job and work after school hours. As an adult, he had power struggles with authority figures and a tendency to be spitefully irresponsible at work.

Needless to say, this limited his success, but on his Saturn return, he began to take a serious look at the effects of his father's death and his own unresolved grief. He was able to take responsibility for the part he played in power struggles with bosses and for the long-repressed resentment at being forced to be an adult before his time. If you or a client are suffering from obstacles in the Saturn areas of life, perhaps a similar analysis can help identify where the blockage comes from. The various healing tools given in other chapters can help identify a strategy for working through the barrier.

It's About Time

With my own Venus Saturn aspect, I often have lucky breaks in timing. As I get older, I more and more sense the perfection of timing in my life and others. All timing is perfect, only our perception, our understanding of it is imperfect, creating frustration. Yet spiritual teachers say time is an illusion, and represents our conscious mind's attempt to create structure and order for our experience. Some say all our lives occur simultaneously, in the Eternal Now.

In our youth-oriented culture, we've all grown to have an inordinate fear of aging. Thus, Saturn's transits and cycles, which generally bring an increased awareness of the passing of time, are more difficult for us than they need to be, more difficult certainly than in cultures and eras where the wisdom and experience of age is appreciated.

A Meditation About Saturn and Time

Breathe slowly and let your muscles relax. Let go of tension. Just slow your breathing down.

Use the ticking of the clock to keep going down deeper into your center. The rhythm of it is like the beating of the heart, beating to its own bodily rhythm. Our lives must be in rhythm, rather than forced in our effort.

Get the sensation that time, while it is important, is really on a continuum, moving continuously forward, so there is always more coming. We can pace ourselves, and know that all will be fulfilled in time.

But just as you cannot hurry the hours in the day, neither can you hurry your own internal timing of when parts of you will develop, and become manifest. Trust that this is in process, just as you trust that surely 8 o'clock will follow 7 o'clock and 9 o'clock will follow 8 o'clock. You do not have to pay attention to it—9 o'clock will simply come of its own accord.

And so, too, will come your further development, peacefully and gradually, without forcing it. You cannot hurry growth, any more than you can make midnight come faster.

The Meaning of Delay—All in the Perfection of Time

We constantly judge ourselves against perfectionistic standards of production, not seeing the wisdom in our seemingly fallow periods. During Capricorn, the ground is at rest and nothing is growing, yet the earth is regenerating itself. In our own intervals of rest, we play, we go over old ground, and we prepare ourselves for the future.

Delay is not an obstacle but an opportunity to get better prepared and work on flaws that could be critical to the overall effort if not removed. We know that Saturn is much connected with time and with patience. When we push ahead impatiently to build what we want when we want it, the Saturn scythe can cut us down most unpleasantly, but even here it is teaching us lessons.

Delays can be used productively to plan how to meet the challenge. Good planning and careful thought can mean the difference between success and failure. You can also use the time to hone the necessary skills to a high level. Generally, the delay means that some part of your act is not together yet. You need to lay a solid foundation for further building to be sound and not easily toppled. Used properly, these delays are often fruitful, for they prepare our minds to function at a higher level of competence. Often people have to gain a new concept of themselves as capable to handle this new challenge. They can use the delay as a time to develop the necessary skills, gather additional information, and practice what they will be required to do.

An acronym for time is Today I Make an Effort. If you're in a three mile marathon, you cannot win it on the first lap. Look up to the people who've been in it longer, learn from them, but don't belittle yourself because you aren't where they are. Rather than judge yourself harshly because you're not there yet, just take one step today; and step by step you'll get there.

I have often observed a process in my clients' lives whereby opportunities arise, and then nothing comes of them for a while or there are seemingly endless delays. They are frustrated and come for a reading to find out when they can expect progress. The astrological correlation of this process is that a transiting planet, often Saturn, goes over a planet, then makes a station nearby and goes retrograde far past the original place. While the outer planets are retrograde, we often move into inner work and preparation. When the planet goes direct again over the same place, the opportunity or one very similar seems to come up again. If this happens to you or to a client, examine the delay carefully and enquire what additional preparation would be needed to be successful at this challenge. Use the retrograde period as a time to get prepared to meet it in earnest.

People who are meant for New Age careers are often frustrated at the seemingly endless delays in getting to manifest their visions. They often feel they are wasting their lives, for up until the Saturn return, sometime between 27 and 29, they often drift from job to job and seem to get nowhere, unlike their age peers who are meant for routine work and who seem to get it all together in their twenties. I see such patterns in those with Uranus, Neptune, and Pluto prominent, especially in the sixth or tenth houses or aspecting the Midheaven. There is wisdom in the delay, for most of us aren't able to handle the energies of those planets wisely until after the Saturn return. Balance, maturity, self-discipline, a considerable experience of life, the capacity to put ego aside, and accumulated wisdom are required for such careers.

Good Luck, Bad Luck, and Planning

Saturn is supposed to be unlucky. So often, however, bad luck is just a matter of bad timing and bad planning. By better planning—in fact, by planning, period—much "bad luck" could be averted. For example, if you know that several appliances in your house are likely to fall apart at any moment because of old age, set up an orderly plan (a budget, even) to replace or repair them before they fall apart. Don't let things take you by surprise if you can help it. If you fail to plan, you plan to fail.

I used to have a rather flighty friend who was always in trouble. Her car was a junker, missing headlights, and prone to breaking down. One day she was stopped for the missing headlight, and when it was discovered that she was driving without a license, she was arrested. Her comment was, "It's just my bad luck." My ill-advised comment was, "No, lady, it's just your bad judgment." Where Saturn is in your chart, you'll have a lot less bad luck if you apply such positive Saturn traits as planning, caution, organization, and self-discipline. Fairly often, the harder we work, the luckier we get.

The Perils of Perfectionism

Helen DeRosis, who has written extremely helpful books on such Saturn problems as fear and depression, recommends that when you feel anxiety or suddenly become depressed, ask yourself which impossible expectations or standards you've set up for yourself. In our own charts, Saturn's location by sign and house may give us clues to what those impossible demands are. For example, Saturn in Gemini people set up the expectation they will always be clever and able to master all things intellectual. Those with Saturn in the 11th house expect themselves to always be a perfect friend, and their friends to respond to them perfectly. Generally, where you are the most perfectionistic, you also have the strongest feelings of inferiority, since the standards are nearly impossible to live up to.

Perfectionism is counterproductive, for studies have shown that perfectionists actually accomplish far less than those who are content to do their best and let go of it. The *Psychology Today* report by David Burns on those studies listed in the bibliography is worth looking up and reading if perfectionism is making your life miserable. If you've got something 90 percent perfect, that's probably enough. Perfectionism leads to sloth and procrastination, out of fear of trying. The expectation of failure to live up to these unreasonable demands in itself leads to a failure to try. (The remedy, LARCH, is excellent for those who fear to fail, so therefore fail to make the effort. BEECH helps those who are overly critical of themselves and others.)

Trying to be perfect is a waste of time. If you spend 17 hours making a one hour job perfect, you're wasting your life. Keep a balance between quality performance and time cost. A very fine book called *How to Get Control of Your Time and Your Life,* listed in the bibliography, has been useful in offsetting perfectionism. It divides tasks into categories of what's important and what is not, listing them as A, B, and C in priority. The book says that we generally spend 80 percent of our time on things that are worth only 20 percent. If you start spending 80 percent of your time on the 20 percent of things that really matter, you'll accomplish much more.

On the other hand, discomfort with imperfection can also lead us to shoot for excellence. That imperfection irritates you until you do something about it and eventually build something rather nice from it, as the oyster uses the grain of sand to build the pearl. The key, then, is finding a balance point between the desire for quality and self-mastery and the other, less constructive end of the Saturn spectrum, perfectionism.

Flower Remedies for Saturn Problems

A number of the remedies seem tailor-made for Saturnian character types. BEECH is for the perfectionist who is critical and intolerant of others, becoming irritated at their faults. It also helps those who are too critical of themselves. OAK is for the brave Saturnian plodder, who struggles on and on despite despair, never giving up. For these folks, life has been hard. ROCK WATER is for Saturnians who martyr themselves in pursuit of an ideal. They are rigid, inflexible, and heavily invested in self-denial. VINE is for those who want to dominate and control. WATER VIOLET people are aloof from others, yet quite capable and involved mainly in their own work. Remedies for fear and depression will be discussed separately in the chapters which follow. Remedies for specific Saturn aspects will be given in the section on aspects which follows.

There are also remedies which seem most suited to Saturn transits. OLIVE, HORNBEAM, and OAK are suited to various degrees of fatigue and stress, in the order given, from lesser to greater. CHESTNUT BUD helps you to learn from your mistakes, rather than repeating the same patterns over and over. MALLOW helps in such Saturn cycle passages as the midlife crisis, fear of aging, menopause, and puberty. THYME has to do with the experiencing of time, so that one can reach into the future or past. It overcomes the feeling that time is moving too slowly and seems to speed things up.

Saturn Aspects

The brief readings given here apply mostly to the difficult aspects to natal Saturn, including the conjunction, square, semisquare, sesqui-quadrate, quincunx, and opposition. Obviously, there are also differences between Saturn square Uranus and Saturn opposite Uranus, but this book is not meant to be a complete catalogue of aspects. The goal of this section is to alert you to the kinds of problems that can arise with a given combination and, most importantly, to the healing tools you can use when blockages occur.

SUN/SATURN: (Sun in Capricorn, Sun in the tenth house) Self-esteem depends on achieving perfection. There is an identification of self and self-worth with work, career, or success. This aspect often shows a father who was cold, critical, authoritarian, and demanding. Nothing the child did was ever good enough. The father may have been older, very successful, or else very ambitious—whether or not he was successful. The person received a double message which produced a great fear of success, for to succeed means to go beyond father and to lose him. The old man may not actually be pleased at being outstripped, for it reinforces his fear of failure and means a loss of authority over the child.

With these aspects and also with Saturn in the fifth house, people can be fearful of being themselves, of realizing their potential, and of being childlike and creative. Growing up, there was an environment in which self-expression was limited and where the child quality was disapproved of, in favor of being a miniature adult. Such people had to emulate the authority figure rather than discover the real self. Flower remedies for opening up creativity are IRIS and INDIAN PAINTBRUSH. Clearing the solar plexus and the throat chakra with green light is also helpful. ZINNIA helps you get in touch with the playful child within.

The person with this aspect who overcomes perfectionism and fear is capable, responsible, and reliable, carrying the cloak of authority with dignity. Clearing the Solar Plexus chakra thoroughly with gold light and blue light would be immensely helpful. Flower remedies that would be useful are SUNFLOWER and SAUGERO which are both excellent for father complexes. MULLEIN helps in fulfilling one's own true potential. ELM is for feelings of inadequacy and LARCH for those who expect to fail so, therefore fail to make an attempt.

MOON/SATURN: (Moon in Capricorn or in the tenth house, Saturn in the fourth, to some extent, Saturn in Cancer) This often depicts a mother who was cold toward the child's need, instead of nurturing. Perhaps she was older and no longer patient with children. Where she had too many responsibilities, she may have demanded the child grow up quickly. One client with Moon in Capricorn told me that her mother's favorite saying was, "I'm not raising children, I'm raising adults."

The mother may have worked or been extremely anxious about survival due to poverty. (The Saturn in Cancer generation of the late 1940s were the children of the children of the Depression.) At any rate, it is likely that the child was born during some sort of Saturn time for the mother—financial hardship or other crisis. Sometimes such children are born on their mother's Saturn return or other aspect to natal Saturn, so each party has Saturn in aspect to the other.

As a result, the person with this aspect may grow up insecure about survival, fearful of deprivation, and anxious about becoming dependent. He or she finds security only in success and achievement—"they can't take that away from me." And yet, there is a double message, for to succeed means to lose mother and any chance of being nurtured. In many cases, the mother was very capable and should have been a career woman, but was prevented by responsibility toward a family. Sometimes with this aspect, the mother's thwarted ambition converts into anxiety for her children to succeed.

Generally, the mother was also fearful of emotions because they got in the way of accomplishment, so the children learned they would not be responded to when they were emotional, and came to maintain strict control over the emotions. The only acceptable emotion was depression, so they learned to covert most other feelings (especially anger) to depression. They discover that they're more likely to get concern from other people when they're depressed than when they're angry, as it is easier for others to handle. The mother herself may have been chronically depressed and anxious. She may have suffered a post-partum depression after the child's birth, which the child soaked up and incorporated. The depression may possibly have been due to the fact that the child's birth tied her down to duty and responsibility and meant loss of the opportunity to follow up on career ambitions.

The person with this aspect who releases insecurity, fear, and depression is solid, responsible, and extremely caring, and might be a professional caretaker of some kind, whether a nurse, teacher, or manager of a residence or hotel. Work on the root chakra would be important, especially with blue light. The chapters on depression and fear which follow will contain many useful healing tools for emotional difficulties common to this aspect. RED CHESTNUT is for the overprotective mother or those who worry too much about others. AGRIMONY is for those who hide emotional torment behind a cheerful facade. SCARLET MONKEYFLOWER and FUSCHIA are for integrating repressed emotions. POMEGRANATE helps heal emotional extremes due to improper childhood nurturing.

MERCURY/SATURN: (Mercury in Capricorn, Saturn in the third house or even sometimes in Gemini) Individuals with this aspect tend to have an inferiority complex about their mental abilities or capacity to communicate. Often, the authority figure who made the person feel inadequate was an older brother or sister with outstanding scholastic abilities. The child was frequently compared to this sibling and found lacking. Sometimes this sibling actually demeaned or ridiculed the child, but often it was just the inevitable superiority of someone several years older who'd already learned more advanced skills in school.

Occasionally, people with this aspect had difficulty reading or pronouncing words, or even stuttered, generally because of tension and pressure from parents or teachers who demanded perfection. As a result, Mercury/Saturn individuals are often convinced they're stupid, including one client of mine who was going for her doctorate in physics. Generally, the minds of such individuals mature with age, and they may actually do better in college or beyond than in high school. They may wind up being intellectuals in old age, when they feel they've earned the leisure time. Albert Einstein, who developed the theory of relativity, was, early in his life, considered retarded because of his slowness in school and in communication skills. He had a close conjunction of Mercury and Saturn in Aries. According to Lois Rodden's *Astro-Data II* Einstein was born March 14, 1879 at 11:30 AM LMT, in Ulm, Germany, 10E00; 48N30.

The Mercury/Saturn chants or rosaries would be good preparation for mental work. Meditation on a specific mantra and deep breathing would also help clear the mind. Flower remedies which would help are WHITE CHESTNUT, for learning from your mistakes, PENNYROYAL, to relieve negative thinking, and LEMON for mental clarity and learning skills such as math or computer. Clearing the brow chakra with blue or white light would also be useful. Like many Saturn aspects, the best healer for this one is time and experience.

VENUS/SATURN: (Venus in Capricorn, or in the tenth house, Saturn in the seventh) Venus/Saturn people often had parents who made them feel they had to EARN love through hard work and success. Thus, Venus/Saturn people often believe that people will only love them if they succeed, but often the opposite is true, especially for women. People are put off by success, unfortunately. There can be loneliness in excellence. In search of success—which is their way of looking for love—these people focus so heavily on work that there is little time or energy for social contact. They wind up shutting people out, too busy to fit closeness into their lives. When they get rejected, they don't understand it…"Why don't you love me? Didn't I produce? You want to see my resume?" Spiritually, Venus/Saturn aspects may be for the purpose of giving you the space to be excellent and the freedom to develop your capabilities, without the distraction and limitation that marriage and family can bring.

True love often comes late to the Venus/Saturn person. But then, love is often better for the mature. When we bring our experience to love and add that to the loved one's experience, then something of worth is built. We have already built a solid foundation under ourselves, have already made many of our mistakes. Young people can be so self-involved that they only relate to others when it touches them. One with more seasoning and more knowledge of the world and life does not expect their lover's world to revolve around them. We have given up expecting miracles of love, no longer expect love to transport us, to transform us, to be the magic ingredient that helps us set the world on fire. We are more realistic, not so dewey-eyed over the Hollywood ending. We are not so easily deceived that lust is love, and we have doubtless had our fill of lust. We look for character, not just for surface Venusian values. We are grateful for the companionship, but have a more solid sense of self. We see the limits to love and are more ready to settle for someone who is just another human being like ourselves.

People talk about a Venus/Saturn aspect as an unlucky Venus, but sometimes it acts as a lucky Saturn. It's like when you have good luck and people say, "You must be living right." I have this aspect and have been extremely lucky with Saturnian things. I have a fine-tuned and fortunate sense of timing. Also, when I do my duty or fulfill my responsibility, good fortune often follows. Duty may not be any fun, but doing it often prepares me for something else, or, in the course of doing it, I "happen on" something else that is positive.

Flower essences for the Venus/Saturn aspect would include BLEED-ING HEART, for lost love, WALLFLOWER for confidence in your own attractiveness, and STICKY MONKEYFLOWER, for fear of intimacy. Others include DOGWOOD, for gentleness and grace in relationships, FIG, for trust between couples, and MARIPOSA LILY, for receptivity to love and healing feelings of alienation and separation. Long, hard work on the heart chakra will no doubt be required, to clear out old sorrows and the fear of giving and receiving love. Blue and pink light in that center would be especially powerful.

MARS/SATURN: (Mars in Capricorn, Mars in the tenth house, Saturn in Aries) There is much fear with this aspect—fear of anger, aggression, asserting yourself, and of sexuality. There can be performance anxiety and fear of failure, which in itself can lead to failure. This aspect is one of the signatures of the abused child, although you wouldn't make such a determination without other confirming aspects. (The chapter on domestic violence in my book, *Healing Pluto Problems*, discusses these signatures at length, with chart examples.) At the very least, the aspect shows stern discipline. The child may have had a brutal or harsh authority figure, who feared his own anger and held it in, or would withdraw until it built up and then would explode. The parent was often repressive toward the child's anger or self assertiveness. The native may repeat the pattern, holding in anger until it explodes, reinforcing the fear of anger, in a vicious cycle. The parent may have been fiercely competitive with the child, reacting hypercritically or punitively toward the child's own strivings for self-mastery and importance.

Remedies for anger include BEECH, IMPATIENS, WILLOW, and HOLLY. CHERRY PLUM is specifically for the fear that anger will get out of control and cause the person to harm themselves or others. Other essences include BORAGE for cheerful courage and TRUMPET VINE for assertiveness. Clearing all the chakras with red light is also useful. LARCH eases the fear of failure.

JUPITER/SATURN: (To a lesser extent, Jupiter in Capricorn or in the tenth house, Saturn in the ninth house or in Sagittarius) The aspect may produce a cautious attitude toward growth, for in the experience of this person, every growth can bring a setback or added responsibilities. These people often experience growth (Jupiter) from doing their duty or other Saturn virtues. Similar to the Venus/Saturn aspect, people with this aspect also often experience "good fortune" from taking responsibility or doing their duty. It shows an excellent capacity to grow and learn from experience.

The parents of such people may have been older—but also wiser. Due to difficult experiences, they could have been afraid to be optimistic, as in the Yiddish saying, "kine hora." The person with this aspect is extremely conscientious, but can also be up-tight, pompous, self-righteous, and judgmental. The child's natural enthusiasm and exuberance may have been squelched. Such a person often grew up in a very serious household which placed great value on education and scholarship, and many of these people are natural scholars, taking pleasure in learning serious things or in serious study of religion or philosophy. Anxiety may come from perfectionism about school performance, which may keep them from achievement in that area until later in life. Not too abstract, the person generally believes learning must have practical applications. Remedies which would be useful for this aspect are ST. JOHN'S WORT, for trust in the divine, PENNYROYAL, for negative thinking, and OPAL, for hope.

URANUS/SATURN: Such people may be afraid of being different and of expressing their individuality, yet are crystallized into doing it compulsively. Due to their hardened yet not immediately obvious defiance, if you tell them what to do, you can be sure it won't get done, or at least not when and how you tell them. Yet, left to their own initiative, they can be extremely responsible. They do best working for themselves. With Saturn aspects to Uranus, the individual is the original marginal man, not fitting anywhere. With conservative people, the rebel or nonconformist position is taken; with the rebel element, the person plays more of a traditionalist. Deeply rebellious against authority, the person is too fearful to show it openly and thus does it in more subtle ways. Left to their own devices, rather than being told what to do, such people can be extremely responsible and capable, very much self-starting.

This pattern develops when parents cling to tradition and yet secretly yearn to break loose, inwardly rebelling against the responsibilities and duties which force them to take the Saturn path. The children are covertly encouraged to be different and to follow their own path. Or, perhaps the parents are very, very different from one another, one Saturnian and one Uranian, and the child was somehow caught between, having to please both. The child may also have been born at a time of mixed messages culturally or during rapid cultural change, when the political climate was conservative, but the forces of change were also active underground. The spiritual purpose of this aspect seems to be to bridge what was once called the generation gap, that is, to find a way for the culture to reconcile the forces of change with the need to preserve what is valuable—to distinguish, if you will, the difference between the baby and the bath water.

Flower essences which would be useful are SAGEBRUSH and MULLEIN, both for establishing and fulfilling one's own identity and true potential. VERVAIN is for those who are incensed at injustices.

SATURN /NEPTUNE: (Less strongly, Saturn in Pisces or the twelfth house, Neptune in the tenth house) Parental and other authority figures may have been inconsistent at best, and alcoholic, severely disturbed, or destructive at worst. These parents did not help the child develop structure, responsibility, and self-discipline, so that the adult can be lacking in these Saturnian attributes. At other times, such children had to be the parent to their faltering parent figures, and so can be excessively responsible, even to the extent of martyrdom. The Saturn return can be a difficult time for either type, providing a difficult confrontation with reality, but these people are stronger afterwards, having more of the positive Saturn traits. The remedies for fear and depression, given in the chapters which follow can be very useful. If there is an alcoholic parent, the Alanon groups for adult children of alcoholics are the best healing of all. (Such groups are also open to adult children of other addicts and to dysfunctional families in general.) Many of the remedies and exercises given in the sections on

Neptune in the second book would be useful, but most especially CORN and MANZANITA, both of which are good for grounding in practical reality.

SATURN/PLUTO: (Less strongly, Saturn in Scorpio, Pluto in the tenth house) An extremely difficult aspect, in that the parents and other authority figures may have been extremely oppressive, controlling, or even corrupt, with very difficult power struggles ensuing. Alternately, there may have been severe hardships which forged this individual into one with the strength of diamonds. (The eras of the Pluto Saturn conjunctions have been difficult times for mankind, for example, 1914-15, 1947-48.) At worst, the person can be extremely rigid, embittered, and self-destructive in relationship to authority, success, and power; at best, the person can be an extremely responsible and self-disciplined healer, researcher, or authority. The series of exercises and tools given in my book, *Healing Pluto Problems,* might be very useful for the individual with this aspect, especially those in the chapter on guilt and resentment, for which the remedies HOLLY, WILLOW, and PINE would be very helpful. WILD ROSE helps with the fear of death.

Helpful Books to Read About Saturn Issues

Burns, David. "The Perfectionist's Script for Self-Defeat." *Psychology Today*, (November, 1980), 34-52.

A lengthy and extremely useful exploration of the perils of perfectionism. Worth a trip to the library, or, if it's not available there, order from Psychology Today Reprints, Box 278, Brooklyn, NY 11205.

Greene, Liz. Saturn: *A New Look At An Old Devil.* York Beach, ME: Samuel Weiser, Inc, 1976.

A treasured exploration of the psychological meanings of Saturn's placements which has helped many readers to grow up and clean up their acts.

Lutin, Michael. *Saturn Signs.* New York: Crown Press, 1975.

Michael Lutin's pungent observations and wit have made him a favorite speaker. The book takes a kind of Dutch uncle look at Saturn's effects in each sign.

CHAPTER FOUR

SATURN AND FEAR:
NEUROSIS OR INNER WISDOM?

Saturn has to do with limits, and anything which causes us to move beyond our limits (or what we BELIEVE are our limits) will bring up fear. Yet, like the rings of Saturn, fears in themselves create limitations. As we look into the fears which limit our lives, we will discover a number of Saturn's negative traits—like negativity, perfectionism, rigidity, and unquestioning acceptance of authority. Just as Saturn has both positive and negative functions, we will find fear also serves positive purposes. Fears that come up with specific Saturn aspects will be discussed. Finally, in keeping with the homeopathic approach, we will consider how Saturn's positive traits—such as planning—can overcome debilitating fears. Healing tools and techniques will be given in the last section of this chapter.

Fear as the Granddaddy of All Neuroses

Fear is awful. When it strikes, we feel vulnerable and helpless. The body contracts, and the heart goes into spasm. The feeling is so uncomfortable, we'll do anything to hide from it. Thus, fear most often wears a mask. In defense, we run into compulsive activities, deaden ourselves by overindulgence, get sick, or freeze into apathy. When these attempts to hide become chronic, they take on the disguise of a PROB-LEM, like a compulsion, addiction, or block. Freud's theory of neurosis stated that symptoms were attempts to relieve anxiety, and that anxiety always derived from repression.

Fear is at the root of many self-defeating behaviors. The person who loses 50 pounds and rapidly gains it back doesn't do so out of lack of will power, but out of terror of what it will mean to be thin. The ghetto-born student who wins a scholarship and then gets pregnant isn't promiscuous but frightened of leaving her people behind to face an unknown world. The promising writer who spends years avoiding the typewriter isn't lazy but scared of failure or of the creative process, which cannot be controlled.

Fear's capacity to create other problems in its wake is the reason for this chapter. If we understand and overcome fear, other difficulties also begin to clear up.

The Positive Functions of Fear

As Seth, the spirit guide in Jane Robert's book *The Individual and the Nature of Mass Events*, pointed out, fears—sometimes even seemingly irrational ones—can awaken the body if you have been too lethargic or in a rut. If you trust your nature, it is easier to trust such feelings.

Seth also noted that fears have a positive origin and a useful purpose. All of them are appropriate at some point in our lives and serve a protective function. Fear is often wisdom arising from self-knowledge. For instance, if you cannot swim and you're afraid to jump off the high diving board, the reluctance is merited. Many times, fear is not neurosis but inner wisdom, warning that you do not have the capability or experience to handle the situation. Inhibitions act as brakes, cautioning us against unwise or even dangerous actions.

Fears keep us from taking on more than we can handle. They are blocks the Higher Self erects to keep us from actions which would be disastrous before we developed sufficient maturity and self-discipline. There are generally good reasons for these feelings, if we analyze them, and thus we should pay attention to them. Inner wisdom is guiding us, sealing doors that shouldn't be opened yet. Saturn is timing, and fear may come from an inner awareness that the time isn't right. We remain immobilized until the proper condition or person appears, without which the effort would fail. Saturn transits often provide the proper conditions or growth for moving through barriers.

Thus, if blocked, get Saturnian. Analyze the concrete steps necessary to do the thing safely and well, and then get to work acquiring the tools or information. Only concrete preparation and disciplined effort can develop the necessary skills. Don't neglect positive Saturnian traits such as planning, preparation, and practice. After that, if you're still too afraid, respect your fear. The timing is not yet right. The preparation isn't wasted, however, because no effort is ever wasted. Your work will make it that much easier to move ahead when it's time. You were practicing, that's all. There is no failure, only successive approximations of the goal.

However, Saturn also shows rigidity and crystallization. Fear may outlast its usefulness and may generalize beyond the original unsafe situation into other similar situations. Excessively anxious parents may short-circuit learning and leave us afraid to try. Perhaps when you were six or seven, fear served to warn of danger, but with age and experience, the situation is no longer beyond you. You learn, get additional skills, and yet the fear remains. The once appropriate warning signal is no longer appropriate. The remainder of this chapter is meant to help overcome fears which unnecessarily limit the way you live.

How Negative Saturnian Attitudes Contribute to Fear

We've noted before how each of Saturn's qualities is on a spectrum from positive to negative. The positive expressions are indispensible to accomplishment; the negative ones make you afraid to try. For instance, the useful attributes of caution and careful assessment can become an immobilizing anxiety. Let's look at how Saturn traits which have shifted down to the negative end of the spectrum contribute to fear. Behind these traits lie certain ideas, so overcoming barriers may require changing attitudes, perhaps by repeated affirmations.

CRYSTALLIZATION: When we are too crystallized into old forms, we're afraid to try something new. Change is a matter of breaking down old patterns and creating new ones. The overly crystallized person is fearful that change means formlessness and lack of structure, rather than trusting more appropriate structures to evolve. Even jellyfish and amoebas have limits to their formlessness.

RIGIDITY: When thinking patterns become too rigid, we tend to resist new ideas. "This is the way it's always been and this is the way it must be." There are many ways to look at any situation, but rigid perceptions and definitions limit our effectiveness at problem solving. If we believe there's only one way, our belief limits us to one method. If that method doesn't work, we're stopped for as long as we persist in thinking that way.

PESSIMISM/NEGATIVITY: One of the greatest obstacles to accomplishment is the self-fulfilling prophecy of failure. Perhaps you did fail at some point, but that doesn't take into account your capacity to learn from mistakes. Greater experience and knowledge enables mature individuals to accomplish things they couldn't do in youth. In fact, areas of your chart touched by Saturn are precisely those where you're a late bloomer. Projections of failure, however, make you afraid to try.

PERFECTIONISM: Perfectionism is a big inhibitor for the Saturnian— and for all of us in the Saturn areas of the chart. Research has shown that perfectionists accomplish far less than those who are able to tolerate mistakes and imperfections. Moreover, perfectionism is highly arrogant.There's hidden conceit that says you're such a rare jewel that you shouldn't have to learn from mistakes like the rest of us mortals. Your efforts, from the word go, should be flawless. This demand paralyzes you, because it's so grandiose as to be impossible, and you're afraid even to try. The only way to get to the top of the mountain without sweating is to be born there.

REVERENCE FOR AUTHORITY FIGURES: Many fears are based on critical judgments by authority figures. We accept their assessments of our abilities as gospel and thus limit ourselves. These authorities, who seem omnipotent to us as children, are fallible human beings, full of fears of their own. Readings later in this chapter demonstrate that many worries were programmed by our parents.

For example, if daddy, for reasons best known to him, grew up scared of sex, he cannot help but communicate that to us, so that it becomes our own fear. If mommy was afraid to let you do anything rugged with your body—who knows, maybe you were a sickly tot—you might see physical activities as dangerous and avoid them. Even though the fear may have been perfectly valid at one point, it continues after it is no longer valid. When your mother was young, death in childbirth may have been very common, and she may have had loved ones die while giving birth. You may have taken on her concern, consciously or unconsciously, and may be afraid to give birth, even though modern methods make it safe. Yet fear creates constriction, so fear of delivery may actually make labor more difficult.

Metaphysics teaches that what we consistently imagine in our minds can be shaped into reality. Saturn is both fear and concrete form, and the fears we dwell on, we can bring into being. Parental prophecies are often self-fulfilling. If Mrs. Smith constantly worries that little Johnny will turn out to be a drunk like her brother, whom he resembles, her behavior communicates this, and his character is formed by that concern. Your parents' fears can ultimately become reality, unless you recognize them as illusion.

In order to stop living out your parents' fears, come to see mom and dad as mortals. Know that what their imagination told them about you twenty years ago has no bearing on the individual you're becoming now, unless you allow those ideas to limit you. It would help to write an inventory of things your parents feared, both for themselves and for you. Your Saturn signs and aspects—as well as theirs—would give clues. (See the delineations later in the chapter for possibilities.)

THE EITHER/OR SYNDROME: In their desire to make everything

concrete and categorizable, Saturnians make fixed judgments about things that aren't fixed at all. A thing is either gold or it isn't, says the Saturnian, and he's right. A thing is either awfully perfect or it's perfectly awful, says the Saturnian, and he's wrong. He thinks he's either good or bad, capable or incapable, deserving or undeserving, and that's his reality, permanent and unchanging, until he's reborn with a whole new chart. Material goods like gold can be measured and graded, but human traits and abilities are relative, changing, and evolving. The Saturnian often leaves no room for evolution—if the first painting isn't museum quality, he's obviously not cut out to be an artist, so there's no point going on. With a judge and jury like that looking over his shoulder, of course he's afraid to try.

Using the Capricorn Rising Wheel to Overcome Fears

For difficulties represented by Saturn, we'd use the wheel for Capricorn, the sign Saturn rules. To understand fear, explore negative traits of signs falling on each of the houses. Then, homeopathically, draw on positive characteristics of the same combinations to find remedies. The principles are true of all of us, regardless of our rising signs. Capricorn rising people, however, are often extremely fearful and cautious. For that reason, people with Capricorn rising may find this exploration especially helpful.

My students discovered a personal application of this wheel. Put your natal planets into a wheel with 0 degrees of Capricorn on the Ascendant, and the houses where natal planets fall have special relevance to your fears. For instance, if you had Saturn and the Sun conjunct in Aries, they would fall into the fourth house of this wheel, and the reading given for the fourth house should have special meaning for you.

CAPRICORN ON THE FIRST HOUSE: With Capricorn on the first, many of the Saturn-related reasons for fear discussed earlier are strongly present. Fear of change and of structure breaking down arises out of rigidity and crystallization. Working on the attitude changes discussed earlier would be helpful. You may be erecting a wall to keep the world at bay. Perhaps you believe you must always appear to have it all together—no runs in the nylons, ladies, or you don't reach the boardroom or the bedroom. You may feel you cannot just go in and flounder around or you'd jeopardize your whole future. Do it right or not at all. The piranhas will get you if you appear uncertain. Attitudes like these heap up mounds of anxiety. Examine your thinking patterns when it comes to the things you are afraid of.

How can you use the postive traits of Capricorn on the first house to overcome fear? Do put your best foot forward in a new or anxiety-producing situation. Dress and look your best. Go slowly, and be well prepared for the occasion by planning carefully. Well begun is half done.

AQUARIUS ON THE SECOND HOUSE: One important insight from Aquarius on the second house is that most fears concern separation. We're afraid of losing something we value, whether it be material goods or relationships. As The Course In Miracles says, NOTHING REAL CAN BE THREATENED. If it's real friendship and not just ingratiation, real talent and not just fantasy, a real money-making idea, a real whatever, then it cannot be threatened by taking a risk.

The remedy is also Aquarian...cultivate detachment from material goods and clinging relationships. Aquarius relates to consciousness, so know that the only thing of permanent value, the only thing you take with you when you die, is consciousness. Rebel against the tyranny of possessions and the idea that your worth is determined by money! Come to value change as an opportunity to expand your awareness and to become even more perfect than you already are.

PISCES ON THE THIRD HOUSE: Vernon Howard, a self-help author says that worry is a burdensome hoax, supplying us with the illusion we are doing something about the situation. Pisces on the third house suggests that most fears are figments of the imagination. We imagine consequences of the projected action, then accept those projections as reality. We imagine others will laugh at us, criticize us, reject us. We imagine we'll lose everything and wind up in the poor house or the hospital. All this is fantasy. Most of the things you worry about will never happen. (An acronym for FEAR is False Evidence Appearing Real.)

The truth of this was brought home once when I was going through a period of anxiety attacks. Someone suggested I keep a worry box, writing fears down on pieces of paper, praying over them, and releasing them. At the end of a month, I opened the box and found 26 pieces of paper. Out of 26 overwhelming worries, each of which had been my total reality for a day or two, only one had actually happened!

One of my therapists used to say, all too frequently for my comfort, that THE FEAR IS THE WISH. That is, our worst fears are also sometimes our best fantasies. Yet these wishes are unacceptable, so we project them onto others. For example, we may be furious at someone (Aries on the fourth house) and wish to harm them, but we turn it around and say they mean to harm us. Or, we want everyone to look at us, but we're brought up modestly, so we distort the wish into fear that everyone will notice what we're doing and disapprove. These distortions don't make any logical sense, but when was Pisces last accused of logic?

If negative of magination creates fears, then positive use can help them. overcome them. Use the technique of visualization to create a positive new mind set, seeing yourself accomplish the thing you're afraid to tackle. Pisces on the third suggests that what's most fearful is that which is mysterious and unknown. Use imagination to think the situation through, in a preliminary exploration of what it might be like. This also serves the purpose of rehearsal, familiarizing you with new conditions.

ARIES ON THE FOURTH HOUSE: At the root of many fears is a kind of Arien self-centeredness—ME, ME, I, I. They will look at ME. I will fail and make a fool of myself, and they'll laugh at ME. We exaggerate our importance in the total scheme of things, when most of the time people simply don't care about or notice what we do. The solution is also Arien/Martian. Take the focus off the self and put it on the goal...the point of the arrow on the symbol for Mars.

Another wellspring of fear is competitiveness. We wish to surpass our parents and authority figures, yet to do so would be construed by the unconscious as an act of aggression against those who nurtured us. We're afraid of making our parents angry, because, in the unconscious, they're still the omnipotent giants they were when we were children. Acknowledge and accept your aggressiveness and competitiveness. What's wrong with them anyhow? It's an act of aggression to get born or to leave mommy behind while you go off to kindergarten, you mean thing you!

Finally, Mars has to do with anger, and at the foundation of fear may be some anger you're not facing. In conflict, all animals mobilize themselves for either fight or flight, and here the flight response has won out. Another acronym for FEAR is F... Everything And Run. Ask what you're angry about—and what you fantasize would happen if you expressed that anger. When you see it for what it is, it becomes less scary. Reading books on anger or taking assertiveness training also can help.

TAURUS ON THE FIFTH HOUSE: The fifth house is risk-taking including such risky endeavors as love affairs, children, creativity, and pleasure. To put the fixed earth sign, Taurus, there means rigidity can get in the way of risking. Use the positive, earthy, practical side of Taurus to take an almost sensual pleasure in your efforts....get dirt on your hands, even under your nails. Use that Taurus serenity to enjoy without judging. Unlike the other earth signs, Taurus is not particularly critical or hard on itself.

GEMINI ON THE SIXTH HOUSE: The hobgoblins of your mind can actually make you ill. Fear creates mental stress, and stress can translate into bodily complaints. When people say they're worrying themselves sick, they're probably telling the truth. How can you use this same combination positively? First, put Gemini's humor to work and exaggerate fear to the point of ridiculousness. If you don't have a sense of humor, then work at that. Second, put the mental agility of Gemini to work, brainstorming for solutions. There are a dozen ways to tackle any task, some much easier than others. No one says you have to do it the hard way. What else? Talk, talk, talk about your fear until it diminishes.

CANCER ON THE SEVENTH HOUSE: The fear that you cannot do things often stems from excessive dependency. Check out intimate relationships for a smotherer who's creating the impression you cannot survive without those tender ministrations. Even when nobody in the present fits that role, many fears go back to the original heavy-duty commitment...mom. What is the way to turn it around? Find some nurturing partners, all right, but only stick with those who allow you to grow and who cheer you on while you do.

LEO ON THE EIGHTH HOUSE: Many a bit of progress has died a premature death on the horns of pride. Pride can get in the way of our best efforts to improve. Conversely, the death of the ego makes most fears needless. That's what they're all about, aren't they? Fear somebody will laugh at you, that you won't look good, that you'll be caught with your pants down...all pride and ego. So how can you turn it around and get rid of pride? Kill it off!

VIRGO ON THE NINTH HOUSE: This combination shows the tendency to shoot down your ideas and efforts before giving them a fair chance. Here, the negativity and perfectionism of Virgo come in. "It won't work so don't try." To capitalize on the positive traits, first let your thoughts flow freely (Pisces on the third house) and then take them apart, in a task analysis of their practicality. Virgo loves to work, and the ninth house is knowledge, so get to work learning all you can about the subject, and you'll feel more confident.

LIBRA ON THE TENTH HOUSE: This combination shows a common yet futile trait which contributes heavily to fear—the desire for everyone in the world to love you. Always. Unconditionally. Many of our fears come out of this terror of rocking the boat. "They won't like me if I do that." Will you remain an immobilized crowd pleaser? Placating authority figures goes with Libra on the tenth, but Libra is the sign of equality, so you can begin to turn that around by seeing bosses and parents as equals.

SCORPIO ON THE ELEVENTH HOUSE: Here fear becomes paranoia and distrust of others. Don't show weaknesses or needs, the thinking runs, or it'll give THEM power over you. Yet fear kept secret grows in strength, while fear communicated with loving friends is transformed. Another positive use of this placement is to use a support group or self-help group to overcome the things you're afraid of.

SAGITTARIUS ON THE TWELFTH HOUSE: Some house positions speak reams about fear. Sagittarius on the twelfth shows a loss of faith or hope—a forgetting of our divine support system and spiritual helpers. It's been said that faith is fear that has said its prayers. Conversely, metaphysical teacher Raymond Charles Barker used to say that fear was misplaced faith—faith in the negative.

Another interpretation of this position—combined with Pisces on the third—is that fear arises when we hide from truth or deceive ourselves or others. Someone (Seth, no doubt) said that ALL ILLNESS IS AN ATTEMPT TO ESCAPE FROM THE TRUTH. There's nothing like a guilty conscience to stir up anxiety. One psychological study showed that people who had the fewest fears were those who were the most honest! Most of the time it's not an outright lie, mind you, just one of those famous Sagittarian exaggerations.

When you're most fearful, ask how you're hiding the truth from yourself or others. Turn that Sagittarian thirst for knowledge loose on the secret, twelfth house wellsprings of fear, and start to find out what's behind it. The twelfth house is a prison, and Sagittarius there says the truth shall set you free!

Saturn Aspects and Fears They Represent

The final section of this chapter contains tools for overcoming your barriers, but first you need to get clear about what they are. To help make an inventory, the following section describes typical fears of Saturn placements. Since the desire to be free of fear is a great motivation, you will doubtlessly notice that in the areas of your greatest fears, you may also have enjoyed your greatest accomplishments. This is especially true after the Saturn return, between 27 and 29, when many get fed up with being held back and decide to do something. People frequently overcome barriers at other points in Saturn's cycles, with key aspects forming every seven years.

SATURN ASPECTING MARS, IN ARIES, OR IN THE FIRST HOUSE: Presents difficulties concerning leadership, competition, anger, and self-assertiveness; fear of taking the initiative and fear that leaders will be as harsh as the repressive parent, usually the father. This aspect is often seen in cases of physical or verbal abuse of children. (Verbal abuse is more likely in the air signs.) At the very least harsh discipline was applied. The person became terrified of expressing anger, lest they be like the brutal role model. There are also inhibitions about physical or sexual activities, or using the body aggressively in sports.

SATURN IN TAURUS OR IN THE SECOND HOUSE: Causes tension about money and financial affairs, feelings that they'll never have enough, no matter how well off they are. Sometimes these individuals grew up in poverty, but the placement doesn't mean they'll be limited financially all their lives—Jacqueline Onassis had it. They are afraid they won't have the status they crave unless they have money and possessions—keeping up with the Joneses as an indicator of their worth. Their parents fantasized winding up in the poor house, so they dealt with money in authoritarian ways. These children were made to feel they weren't capable of earning it. Tension leads to stricture, so they don't keep money flowing and can even become miserly.

SATURN ASPECTING MERCURY, IN GEMINI, OR IN THE THIRD HOUSE OR CAPRICORN ON THE THIRD: Manifests as an inferiority complex about intellectual matters, which can masquerade as an anti-intellectual stance. This aspect sometimes manifests as stuttering or difficulty with pronunciation, because of tension about communicating, or as the fear that they won't be understood. These individuals may exhibit stage fright about speaking in public or tension about written communications, which are often handed in late, out of worry they won't be perfect. Saturn in Gemini folks have a terminal fear of boredom; they will go to any lengths to avoid boredom, carrying a suitcase of books along on vacation.

SATURN ASPECTING THE MOON, IN THE FOURTH HOUSE, OR IN CANCER, SOMETIMES MOON IN CAPRICORN: Produces pronounced insecurity, manifesting in fearful attachment to home, family, mother, or food, all of which they worry will be snatched away. This person may have been raised by a deeply insecure parent (usually the mother) who transmitted great concern about survival. Sometimes there was a loss or threat of loss in early life. The person may cling to tradition or habit out of fear of change, fear of emotional expression, so the only safe feeling is depression. (The chapter on depression should be useful.)

SATURN ASPECTING THE SUN OR IN LEO: Presents a lack of

self-confidence, worry about not being good enough, so the ego gets attached to being perfect. These people believe they're not worthwhile unless successful and recognized, yet they are also afraid the attention they crave might expose their imperfections. The result is stage fright, performance anxiety. A parental figure, usually the father, was demanding and could never be satisfied. They have a fear of ridicule or humiliation.

With SATURN IN THE FIFTH HOUSE, there is worry about children, which are seen as a heavy responsibility. There is much tension about the need to be the perfect parent and to have the children turn out perfect. They are inhibited about the child within, therefore also about creative self-expression, which takes too much time away from serious pursuits like career or family responsibilities. When INDULGED in the creative effort needs to be perfect—museum quality.

SATURN IN VIRGO OR IN SIXTH HOUSE, CAPRICORN ON THE SIXTH: Causes individuals to fear that they're not perfect in their work and that they'll lose their jobs. They are fearful they're not going to succeed in work, or not working hard enough. They use workaholism to offset other anxieties; may have had critical, driven, workaholic parents. Persistently worried about health matters, diet, and hygiene, even to the point of hypochondria or excessive concern about cleanliness.

SATURN ASPECTING VENUS, IN CAPRICORN OR IN THE SEVENTH HOUSE, CAPRICORN ON THE SEVENTH: Manifests as deep fear of getting close, because they'll be found imperfect. They are afraid that they might be abandoned or lose the one they love, so they are threatened by new or potential relationships. A horror of rejection and a belief that relationships will entail too much responsibility, may cause them to run from commitment or choose only people who cannot be committed to them. They believe they aren't good enough to be loved unless they're successful. Once established, they become concerned that people don't love them for themselves, but are using them for their status.

SATURN ASPECTING PLUTO, IN SCORPIO, OR THE EIGHTH HOUSE: Extremely oppressive and even abusive authority figures left them fearful of power and domination. They feel that in order to survive, they have to be their own authority and never let anyone else gain control. They may also fear loss of control through sexuality, with its considerable power, and they are convinced that emotional vulnerability will enable others to manipulate them. Pregnancy and childbearing may be viewed as life-threatening. A parental figure's death or life-threatening illness may have so frightened these individuals that they live their lives in fear of dying.

SATURN ASPECTING JUPITER OR IN THE NINTH HOUSE, SATURN IN SAGITTARIUS: An inferiority complex about education and advanced studies leads to a fear of engaging in them. This person may overcompensate, becoming an expert or scholar. He or she can be afraid to hope, like the Yiddish expression kine hora—if they don't go around hoping, they won't be so vulnerable to the evil eye or fate. They are afraid to take risks; they take calculated risks only and hedge their bets.

SATURN ASPECTING THE MIDHEAVEN, IN CAPRICORN OR THE TENTH HOUSE: Appears as a great concern about career, work performance, and success. The fear of a patriarch who demanded nothing less than perfection results in a fear of bosses and other authorities. These people have extremely high standards, so terror of failure may immobilize them. They are also afraid of success in equal proportion, because of the responsibilities it entails.

SATURN ASPECTING URANUS, IN THE ELEVENTH HOUSE OR AQUARIUS: Causes a fear of expressing individuality. Such individuals sit on the fence—radical versus conservative. They are afraid to express individuality, lest they suffer the consequences of being different. They fear not fitting in anywhere, if their true selves are shown. They are afraid of losing their freedom, yet scared of being free, as freedom leaves them without structure.

With Saturn in the eleventh house, there may have been difficulties with the peer group, where they were too formal and too old for their age, so they weren't popular. As adults, this heritage leaves them shy about reaching out, believing they won't be accepted. They are fearful of losing the few friends they do have, so they'll go to any lengths to keep them. They exhibit social insecurity and shyness about being in groups, because they fear losing their individuality in a group.

SATURN ASPECTING NEPTUNE, IN PISCES, OR IN THE TWELFTH HOUSE OR NEPTUNE IN THE TENTH: There is great confusion between reality and fantasy, leading to nameless anxieties and worries about things that aren't real. Often a parent was alcoholic, emotionally disturbed, or chronically ill. The children were left with realistic concerns about survival and had to operate as adults in a terrifying, shifting reality. They are still confused and fearful as adults, especially of taking on responsibilities they aren't up to, since they had overwhelming duties when they were far too young. They may be extremely rigid, just to keep a grip on things, or may drink or take drugs to relieve anxiety. They may worry about losing their minds. There is fear of psychic talents or of being swallowed up in spiritual seeking that gets out of balance. This difficult aspect gets better after the Saturn return, when Saturn outweighs Neptune.

The Healing Crisis of Anxiety

The following section contains healing tools you can use to break through barriers. There are several things to remember. First, as we discussed at the beginning of the chapter, fear serves a useful function. It was there to protect you at some stage of growth, so be grateful to the part of yourself which created it. Have a dialogue with the fear, to find out why it was there and if its reasons for being still hold true. (The inventory work which follows will help you to get in touch with those reasons.) Recognize that there are things you're afraid of that you still OUGHT to be afraid of. Be gentle with yourself; don't force down a barrier that's there for your own protection. Recognize also that anxiety is often concomitant with growth, that there is energy released in the growth process which may be registered as fear. Accept it as a by-product of growth, and sit with it, for growth is on the other side.

We spoke in an earlier chapter about the healing crisis that often arises when you tackle a problem area. Specifically, tackling fears may temporarily bring them to the surface, so you may feel, for a few days, more frightened than ever. You experience a catharsis that can help you clear out fear and get moving. With Pisces on the third, fear is largely an illusion, so thought patterns surface for you to observe and see how irrational they are, rather than allowing them to immobilize you. In particular, the NEGATIVITY of your thoughts may rise to new heights."This won't work. I cannot. I'll always be a failure." Be conscious of these thoughts, but don't buy into them. Instead, immediately replace them with positive affirmations. The fight or flight response that arises to mobilize you for action is coming up, but you have the opportunity to make a new choice, to fight rather than run.

Recognize also that part of the "fear" you are feeling is actually EXCITEMENT. They are next door to one another on the color wheel of emotions, and we often confuse them, because we don't know how to handle excitement. When you try something new and you feel afraid, ask yourself, "How much of this is actually excitement?" Allow yourself to feel how exciting it is to master yourself and move ahead.

Inventory Work on Fears

Make a list of five things you'd like to do but fear holds you back. Make an inventory of character traits that may play into the fears— pride, passivity, people-pleasing, wanting to feel in control of the situation all the time, or rigidity. Ask yourself the following questions. Writing about them can give you clarity, surprising insights, and direction on how to proceed.

Which one of these is true: I cannot do it or I WON'T do it? How does not being able to do it serve me? For example, does it let me be dependent on others or entitle me to extra care and attention?

What false image of myself and my capabilities am I trying to maintain? How does the expectation of always looking like I have it together keep me from trying something new? Do I fear I'd be expected to function perfectly in this respect all the time?

What do I think I could lose by trying? How does the idea that nothing real can be threatened apply to this situation?

What do I fear would happen if I did this?

What fears did my parents or other crucial adults have for themselves in this area? What fears did they have for me?

Recognizing that this fear was appropriate and protected me at some stage, what purpose did it serve me earlier? How have I changed since then so that I could do this more safely now?

Did I try this when I was younger and fail? If so how have subsequent growth and experience prepared me to succeed at it now?

What new skills or information would I need to do this thing successfully? Are there courses or books to teach me?

Who do I know who could teach me how to do this? What supports could I call on from friends or groups I belong to?

Is pride getting in my way, keeping me from asking for help? Am I afraid of looking foolish?

Do I block myself by insisting I shouldn't have to learn, but instead should be perfect on the first try?

Am I angry about something to do with the situation, down underneath it all? What am I angry about? What do I fear would happen if I expressed my feelings?

Visualizations and Affirmations for Saturn

Once you've used the inventory above to identify where your fears are coming from, visualizations and affirmations are especially important for overcoming Saturn's negativity. Patterns formed in Saturn areas of life are especially tough to change, given Saturn's rigidity. Thoughts that are crystallized require disciplined repatterning. Some general affirmations are printed here, but you may wish to adapt them for your own purposes. Design affirmations for overcoming your own specific fears. Remember to phrase them entirely in positive terms, since negative statements (ones that include no, not, or don't) only wind up reminding your subconscious of the fear.

Design visualizations for specific things fear blocks you from doing. Envision yourself going through one of the situations you've wanted to try. Break it down into small steps and see yourself succeeding at each one. For example, if you've always wanted to paint, see yourself signing up for a painting class, attending it working on a painting, and completing it. See it hanging beautifully framed on the wall and your friends and family complimenting you. Repeat the visualization daily, until you feel the "I cannot's" subsiding and yourself moving forward.

Affirmations For Overcoming Fear:

The causes of my fear are revealed to me, along with solutions.

I move forward at my own proper pace.

I replace fear with confidence in my ability to grow.

I treat myself gently as I move through my fears.

The support I need to move forward are available to me.

I accept my mistakes as part of the learning process.

I accept success in this endeavor as my right.

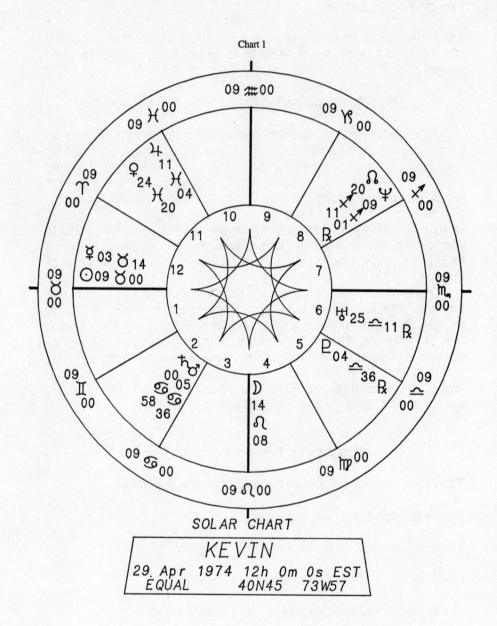

Chart 1

SOLAR CHART

KEVIN
29. Apr 1974 12h 0m 0s EST
EQUAL   40N45   73W57

Deliberate Failure As a Tool

Terror of making mistakes was tormenting a child we'll call Kevin, a bright and appealing seven-year-old referred to me at the psychiatric clinic. Although he was the smartest child in the class and a walking encyclopedia of facts, Kevin would panic each time the teacher introduced a new unit. He would throw himself on the floor, crying like a baby. Obviously, at the age of seven, he'd be having a Saturn square to its original position. He further clued me into this by spontaneously drawing me a picture of the planet Saturn. His time of birth was not available, but he was born on 4/29/74, and his solar chart is shown here as Chart 1. It has a Mars Saturn conjunction in insecure Cancer, squared by Pluto in Libra. With this combination, there is extreme fear of failure, coupled with the belief that it might cause him to lose his mother's love.

The treatment strategy I hit upon to allay Kevin's fear of failure was to have him fail deliberately. Each week, I made up a test of extremely simple material, but the only way he could get an A on it was to get 100 percent wrong answers. We would prepare for the test by rhythmically clapping and chanting, "I don't have to be perfect. It's okay to make a mistake." Then I would correct the test sternly, shaking my head, making big red check marks over each wrong answer as he giggled delightedly. I would proudly display his failures on my office wall. After a couple of months, Kevin no longer threw tantrums in class and was much more relaxed.

The solution, although intuitively arrived at, was homeopathic—using failure to cure the fear of failure. Perhaps you can adapt the same idea to overcome some of your own fears. It especially helps with the fear of looking ridiculous if you fail or make a mistake. The worst has already happened, so you can go ahead and try.

Color Work for Saturn

A university study found blue to be a calming color. Thus, color psychologists confirm the occult teaching that blue is the color of clarity, working to overcome fear. Remember that Pisces is on the third house of the Capricorn Rising wheel, showing that the unknown and mysterious are the most frightening and that fear is often illusion and mental confusion. You can keep calm by working with blue light on the inner level—as well as wearing blue clothing, surrounding yourself with blue walls or textiles, or even using blue light bulbs. Drinking blue solarized water (water which has set for a day in the Sun in a blue glass container) is also calming. The meditation which follows helps clear and center your mind when you're overcome by fear. The inner light color which is most helpful is cobalt blue, like a Vicks "Vapo-rub" jar.

Exercise for the Relief of Anxiety

Create around yourself a bubble of blue light, and fill your body with it as well.

Put a ball of deep blue fire into your solar plexus; let it spin there for a while burning out lack of self-confidence. Then let it spread throughout your body, especially into your brain.

Feel that your whole body and your chakras are melting. They melt down and become a blue pool in the bottom of your bubble.

Look into the blue pool and gradually let yourself become as still as it is.

When you feel calm again, dissolve the bubble.

Saturn Rosaries and the Fears They Heal

In the chapter on healing tools, we described chants and rosaries for difficult aspects. These tools are especially good in healing fears, because repetitive chanting slows down obsessive thinking and helps calm and center you. The table printed here shows how to construct rosaries for various Saturn aspects, what the chants would be, and what fears they counteract, athough the list is not exhaustive. Remember that you cannot use a rosary unless the two planets are connected in your chart, even just by house position. (For instance, Saturn in the twelfth or in Pisces would be like a Saturn/Neptune aspect.)

Saturn Rosaries and Fears They Relieve

ASPECT:	BEAD PATTERN:	CHANT:	FEARS THEY HEAL
SATURN/	RED	OH HAY YAH	Inferiority complex;
SUN	RED	OH HAY YAH	that you aren't good
	BROWN	DAH TI KAH	enough; fear of self-expression.

SATURN/	WHITE	SI IDRIAH	That home, food, or
MOON	WHITE	SI IDRIAH	roots will be snatched
	BROWN	DAH TI KAH	away; insecurity; fear
			of expressing
			emotions.

SATURN/	PURPLE	OH HI TI NAH	Of speaking or
MERCURY	PURPLE	OH HI TI NAH	writing; of school and
	BROWN	DAH TI KAH	tests; of intellectual
			inferiority.

SATURN/	GREEN	NAH TI NAH	Of closeness and
VENUS	GREEN	NAH TI NAH	intimacy; of loss of
	BROWN	DAH TI KAH	love; of not being
			attractive.

SATURN/	BLACK	NAY ZI DAY	Of anger, competition;
		HOH HI MAH	
MARS	BLACK	NAY ZI DAY	of taking action; of
		HOH HI MAH	
	BROWN	DAH TI KAH	sexuality.

SATURN/	YELLOW	HI SU MAI	Of scholastic failure;
		YOH	of intellectual
JUPITER	YELLOW	HI SU MAI	inferiority; lack of
		YOH	faith.
	BROWN	NAH TI KAH	

SATURN/	BROWN	DAH TI KAH	Of being compelled to
URANUS	BROWN	DAH TI KAH	conform; of authority;
	SILVER	AH MITRIAH	of being different.

SATURN/	BROWN	DAH TI KAH	Of psychic and
NEPTUNE	BROWN	AH TI KAH	spiritual experience; of
	MINT	OH MYS	insanity; of illness or
			hardship.

SATURN/	BROWN	DAH TI KAH	ONLY of your own
PLUTO	BROWN	DAH TI KAH	death or someone
	NATURAL	TI OH	else's; of mediumistic
			experiences.

Flower Remedies for Fear

The Bach remedies were developed around 1930, in the climate of fear related to the Great Depression, so there are remedies against a whole spectrum of fears. ASPEN is for anxiety of unknown origin, while MIMULUS is for the fear of something specific. It also helps with general timidity and shyness. LARCH is for people who are afraid of failure, therefore fail to try. ROCK ROSE, an ingredient in Rescue Remedy, is for panic and terror. It's very successful against stage fright and pre-examination panic. In any crisis, you can benefit from RESCUE REMEDY itself, which most health stores carry, even those who don't carry the Bach flower kit. WHITE CHESTNUT is useful for persistent unwanted thoughts, worries, or preoccupations. Among the more modern remedies, BORAGE is for cheerful courage and GARLIC is for releasing fears, insecurities, and nervousness such as stage fright.

You wouldn't want to use more than two or three of the concentrates at a time, as the feelings that come up might be too intense and defeat your purpose. When preparing these remedies, imagine blue light energy coming down from your Higher Self, flowing through your heart center, and through your hands, charging the water in the bottle. Clearly visualize the individual drops of the water glowing with blue light. If you have a tiny chip of quartz crystal, which is associated with Saturn, to put in the bottle or a chunk to place next to it,this would enhance the working of the drops. Blue solarized water would be excellent to use in diluting the concentrated remedies. Use Saturn affirmations or a visualization each time they are taken.

A One Week Blitz on a Specific Fear

If you're ready to tackle a fear or something you've wanted to do but have felt blocked, set aside seven days to work on it intensively. Seven is Saturn's number, and in one week you could make substantial progress in removing the blockage. Saturday (Saturn's day) would be the right day for the culmination of your efforts, so begin on Sunday. If you know how, calculate what hour Saturn would be rising, culminating, or setting. Keying the work into a specific Saturn transit related to that area of life would intensify the process—but if you wait until the PERFECT transit comes along, you'll delay needlessly. If you're new to astrology and don't know when these suggested times are in effect, go ahead and get started, rather than procrastinating.

You might get some flower remedies, especially MIMULUS or ROCK ROSE. Take the diluted remedy four times a day, especially before meditations or inventory work. Do a written inventory, asking yourself the questions listed earlier and any others that occur to you, filling your brain with blue light beforehand. Make a concrete plan, starting with a task analysis, and breaking the undertaking down into specific steps and goals. Set dates or deadlines for accomplishing those goals.

Go to a library or bookstore and get how-to or self-help books on the subject. READ THEM! If there are meditation or subliminal tapes, buy them and use them each day. Do at least one of the meditations above daily, along with visualizations and affirmations designed specifically for the project. Wear as much blue as possible, maybe even treating yourself to something new in that color. Wear or hold the Saturn stone, chant the Saturn chant, and make yourself a rosary.

A Bibliography of Helpful Books About Fear and Anxiety

De Rosis, Helen, M.D. *Women and Anxiety.* New York: Dell, 1981.

Also the author of a valuable book on that other Saturn problem, depression, De Rosis focuses on understanding and on practical tools for overcoming this crippling state of mind.

Ellis, Albert, Ph. D. and William Knaus, E.D. *Overcoming Procrastination.* New York: Signet Books, 1986.

A major barrier to accomplishment is procrastination, which comes out of fear and the desire for perfection. Tools for overcoming it.

Neuman, Frederick, MD. *Fighting Fear.* New York: Bantam, 1986.

An eight week program for treating your own fears and phobias, with some valuable insights into where they come from.

Rubin, Theodore Isaac, MD. *Reconciliations: Inner Peace in an Age of Anxiety.* New York: Berkeley Publications, 1983.

One of Rubin's many excellent self-help books, this one spells out ways of coming to terms with the anxiety and turmoil we experience in living in today's society.

Tec, Leon, MD. *The Fear of Success*. New York: Signet, 1986.

An analysis of where the fear of success comes from and ways to break through these self-created barriers.

CHAPTER FIVE

BEATING THE BLUES: ASTROLOGICAL INSIGHTS INTO DEPRESSION

Depression—the kind that comes for supper and then moves in to stay—is a serious mental health problem. It is as common as the cold, yet can linger for months or even years. In its more serious forms, it is destructive to life, health, and happiness. Other serious problems, such as alcoholism or workaholism can be misguided attempts to cope with long-standing depression. Astrologers link depression to the planet Saturn. If we look at the qualities related to Saturn and at the Capricorn Rising wheel, we will understand more about the causes of this illness, and we will also get ideas about how to relieve it, through the homeopathic principle. Flower remedies and other natural tools will be given.

How to Know if You're Seriously Depressed

The symptoms of clinical depression, as described in various psychiatric texts, fit the traits of the Capricorn Rising wheel surprisingly well. With Capricorn on the first house, the appearance is melancholy. Aquarius on the second testifies that the reaction is often triggered by loss of something valued, but depressed people also find that things which were once important no longer have any meaning. Pisces on the third shows that these people feel confused, disillusioned, and self-pitying. They hide from others, not wanting to communicate. In fact, there are no words to explain how they feel. They may drink, overeat, or use narcotics to deaden the painful thoughts. Aries on the fourth goes along with the well-known principle that underneath and subtly permeating everything is anger. With Taurus on the fifth, overspending may become a way of compensating for the losses. (When the going gets tough, the tough go shopping.)

With Gemini on the sixth, the mental condition is such that concentrating on work is difficult, or conversely, the person may work compulsively to keep the adness at bay. The individual may become hypochondrical or obsesses about health. Colds, pneumonia or lung problems are metaphysically symptomatic of deep sorrow. Cancer on the seventh shows the tendency to regress into dependency. Leo on the eighth can be self-destructive and may manifest in a dramatically expressed death wish. As you would expect with Virgo on the ninth, there is a loss of faith and a critical examination of former beliefs. God is revealed as imperfect.

Libra on the tenth shows the individual is immobilized and indecisive about goals. The manifestation of Scorpio on the eleventh is that there is a retreat into isolation, and a feeling of being all alone, with resentment towards former intimates who are not facing the same problem and who do not understand. With Sagittarius on the twelfth, hope, joy, and faith are gone, and the person may indulge in destructive excess to hide from the pain.

Negative Traits of Saturn and How They Contribute

Just as exaggerated or negative expressions of Saturn contribute to fear, we will find that they also play a part in the development of depression. This is true of people who chronically suffer from depression, as those with a strong Saturn in the natal chart tend to do, as well as those who are suffering from a one-time depression in reaction to some specific event or Saturn transit.

PERFECTIONISM: The demand for perfection is a common attitude with Saturnian people, and for all of us in the areas of life Saturn touches. In her excellent volume, *The Book of Hope,* Dr. Helen DeRosis says depression-prone people alternate between the perfect self and the despicable self. Such people feel they must either be perfect in every respect all the time or they're despicable, awful, nothing. Somewhere along the line, the positive Saturn concern for quality becomes perverted into a tool for self-flagellation. To the helpful desire for excellence, the perfectionist has added the negative elements of compulsivity, rigidity, and intolerance. Those afflicted with depression could benefit from her book, which contains many helpful suggestions for breaking out of this syndrome.

ANXIETY: DeRosis views depression as an addiction, whose primary purpose is to deaden anxiety (another Saturn problem). Anxiety in turn comes from our perfectionistic standards, which are impossible to meet. Use the tools in the chapter on fear to help identify and transcend the fears and limitations you're depressed about.

AMBITIOUSNESS: A Capricorn who is going nowhere is a miserable person. We are all ambitious in the areas where we have Saturn or Capricorn, and we get depressed when we aren't getting anywhere or when we suffer a setback to our hopes and plans. The excessively Saturnian person, however, bases self-worth on achievement, and thus readily turns to self-hate when a plan fails to materialize.

One double Capricorn youngster was afflicted with dyslexia, and was already seriously depressed by the age of eight. He had absorbed much from television about success and affluence and knew already that his inability to read, combined with his family's poverty and the area's lack of facilities for his handicap, meant severely limited prospects. His chart is reproduced here as Chart 2 for astrology students who wish to learn more about dyslexia and about depression. The conjunction of Sun, Moon, and Mercury in Capricorn in the eighth house coincided with his depression, which by adolescence had progressed to the depth of a death wish. The signature of the dyslexia appears to be the quincunx from Mercury to his Gemini Ascendant, which it rules, as well as squares to the Ascendant from Pluto and Chiron.

Depression Itself As A Healing Process

We've spoken previously of the homeopathic principle that symptoms are a sign of health, of the entity's attempts to mobilize its defenses and heal itself. Depression is the body's biochemical demand for time to rest and recover. Transcendental meditation has been recommended to stimulate the body's natural ability to recover by providing the rest the body needs to replace chemical resources depleted by anger, fear, and chronic stress.

Within this framework, depression can be seen as a healing process, a cycle, which consists of a natural reaction to loss. In such cases, it is referred to as reactive depression. If you allow yourself to mourn the loss and go though the process, you don't have to stay there for long periods of time. The book *The Secret Strength of Depression,* listed in the bibliography, discusses in depth the way that allowing yourself to be sad after a loss can keep you from chronic depression.

The sadness is frequently a reaction to facing reality, especially the reality of your own limitations. It comes with those head-on collisions with the material plane we're subjected to from time to time with Saturn transits. Many things about reality ARE sad, and feeling that sadness is an important part of coming to terms with it. We get a little smarter through these confrontations—sadder but wiser.

Saturn is a time-marker, but doesn't have to be depressing unless you're only marking time. The Saturn cycle is the aging process, in which

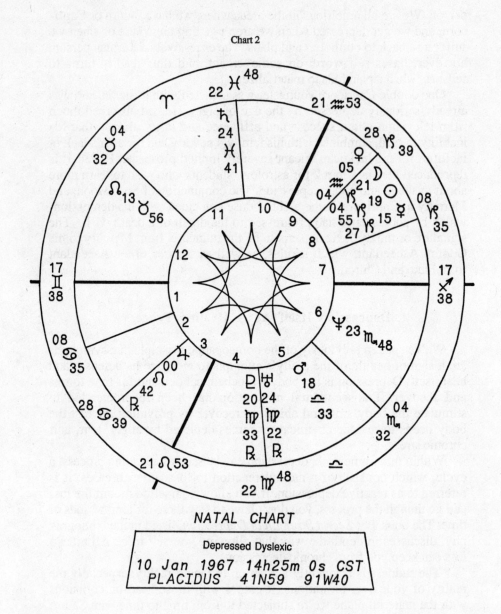

NATAL CHART

Chart 2

Depressed Dyslexic
10 Jan 1967 14h25m 0s CST
PLACIDUS 41N59 91W40

we face up to the limitations time and age place on our youthful hopes and idealism. It makes you foce the fact tha time is passing, that you're getting older, but that can be good. It can be a prompter that brings you back to earth and makes you see that if you want to accomplish things you'd better get with it. Depression is the stimulus that mobilizes you to get to work.

To understand the process and help it along, start at the ascendant and go around the wheel. Many of us get stuck at the third house—Pisces—because we're afraid of anger and more comfortable doping ourselves up. With Aries on the fourth, it is reaching bottom and getting angry that ultimately mobilizes us to action, but action cannot come before the sadness has been fully expressed. If depression is a problem for you, put your natal chart into the wheel to learn more about the places in which you're stuck. Which houses people get stuck in depend on emphasis of the houses of the natal chart, especially the Saturn placement.

Saturn and the Letdown Phenomenon

We've been talking about depression which comes from blocked goals or facing realistic limitations. Yet there's another kind which psychologists call the letdown phenomenon. You've been driving hard to make a goal, and when the big day is over, you go into a slump. This is a common reaction, whether the accomplishment is a college degree or a dinner party for all your friends. The letdown may last only a few days or may become as serious as the reaction many people experience after a major success, like writing a book. Very often, the higher the peak, the lower the slump. We're funny creatures, aren't we? We get depressed if we fail and also if we succeed! But what is the letdown after success related to? It corresponds to a number of the traits of Saturn we've already discussed.

GOALS AND LACK OF GOALS: When you're aiming for a goal, your life has meaning. There is a direction, a purpose, a structure around which everything else is organized. Once you achieve it, there may be a sense of purposelessness. When you have a goal, that Saturnian drive at least has something to be channeled into. When the goal isn't there any more, you have nothing to work toward, nothing to push yourself for. It is as much of a loss as if someone you loved disappeared from your life.

Saturn and its sign Capricorn have to do with mountains, and when you finally get to the top of the mountain, everything else seems flat. When Elvis Presley, who was a Capricorn, died, one radio announcer said, "Well I guess there just weren't any more mountains for him to climb." Elvis had Sun, Mercury, and Venus in Capricorn, as well as a conjunction of Saturn to his Moon, so we may guess that his life-long excesses were undertaken in an attempt to escape depression.[2]

A Saturn remedy for the void created by the loss of a goal is to have another project waiting in the wings, preferably a pleasurable or professionally satisfying one. As you're working on the original goal, keep the next one in mind. Gather information related to it, jot down notes and ideas as you go along, and begin collecting the necessary materials. In this way, your next project will begin to take shape before you've finished the original one. After your big success, you can take a few days to rest and cherish your accomplishment, knowing you still have something to put all that drive to work on.

BIG DADDY IS DEAD: A friend of mine with Moon in Capricorn and Saturn in the first house became seriously depressed when she got her Ph.D. In reaching this life-long goal, she surpassed her mother, who only had a college degree. Saturn is related to authority figures, and one of the problems about getting to the top of the mountain is that you pass a lot of people on the way. You may surpass those you originally looked up to—teachers, bosses, and others you once thought wise and powerful. Saddest of all is leaving your family behind and going on to do things they cannot understand. Rather than making you happy, this circumstance leaves you without comforting, omniscient authority figures—no big mommy and daddy to shield, guide, and protect you. You feel lonely and insecure, and may mourn the loss of that security.

This is a tough problem. The Saturn remedy might be to cultivate a mentor or develop ties with successful people, in your own field and others. If ego and competitiveness isn't allowed to get in the way, association with other winners can provide a mutual exchange of support and valuable information on an equal level. You can understand each other and the stress and loneliness success brings.

REALITY VERSUS EXPECTATION: Pisces on the third house suggests the role that fantasy—and vision—plays in fueling our ambitions. In order to prepare for that big climb, we convince ourselves that if we can just get there, our lives will be magically transformed. We'll have love, popularity, and relief from all our problems. We live with the myth that, "when I accomplish thus and so, then I'll be happy." "If I could only…" or "When I…"

The result cannot live up to the potential we dreamed of. The word potential comes from the Latin word potens, which means power. We think our goal will make us more powerful than the reality proves to be. We equate success with happiness, and when success doesn't instantaneously solve all our problems and meet all our needs, we get depressed (read angry). The top of the mountain is just a little point in space, and a

Chart 3

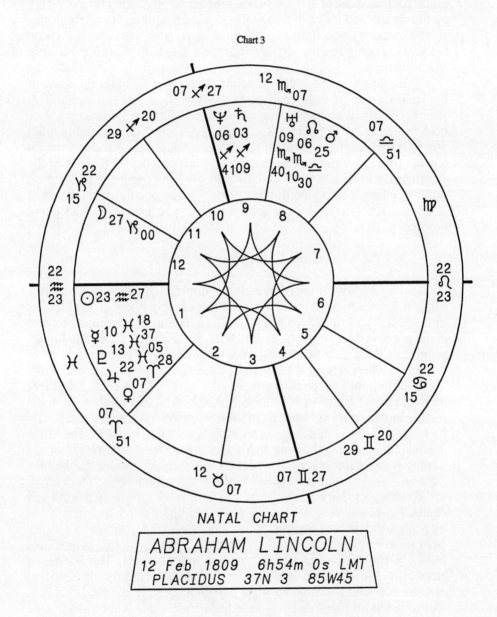

NATAL CHART

ABRAHAM LINCOLN
12 Feb 1809   6h54m 0s LMT
PLACIDUS   37N 3   85W45

rather confining one at that. Achieving the actual goal often means giving up the dream, and its painful to replace a dream with reality. Perhaps this is why so maney stop short of success--at some level, we know our vision isn't real. Hating to give up the fantasy, we stop before getting too close to achievement.

Since Saturn is the reality principle, a Saturn remedy for this facet of the letdown is to be more realistic in the first place, rather than build up your expectations so high. Keep your perspective on what reaching your goal will actually do for you. Getting a Ph.D. won't automatically bring you love and fame, but it ought to get you a better job, and that's reason enough to do it. On the other hand, with Pisces on the third house of the Capricorn wheel, it's your dreams that give you strength to keep on pushing, whereas being totally realistic might keep you down at the foot of the mountain. Better a little letdown when you get there, than going nowhere at all.

Case Examples To Study

History's most famous depressive is doubtlessly President Abraham Lincoln, known to have suffered from bouts of melancholy all his life. His birth chart is shown here as Chart 3. The Moon in Capricorn is prone to depression in the first place, but it is placed in the twelfth house, suggesting deep sorrow deriving from early hardships and deprivation of nurturing, wherein he was made to be excessively responsible as a child. The twelfth house Moon also suggests the possibility of some hereditary or biochemical factor in his illness, possibly from his mother. Both his mother and his wife suffered from illnesses, physical and emotional, and he seemed to have felt deeply responsible to take care of them. The Moon is squared by Mars, showing that anger was prone to be repressed by turning it into depression. The Mars is in Libra, suggesting that he may have been angry over the responsibilities he had to undertake to feel loved.

Hard aspects between Neptune and Saturn are extremely painful and depression-prone, especially when close and highlighted, as Lincoln's is by being conjunct just degrees off the Midheaven. The Midheaven shows what we are remembered for, as he is remembered for his role as the Great Emancipator, which must have rested heavily on him. The combined keywords for Neptune and Saturn are religious duty or spiritual responsibility, all the more so when the ninth house is involved. Lincoln was a man of his times and may have had considerable feeling about what was then called The White Man's Burden.

Our second example is one of the most publicized depressions in recent history. Senator Thomas Eagleton was nominated in 1972 as a vice-presidential candidate for McGovern, only to have a scandal erupt when it was

Chart 4

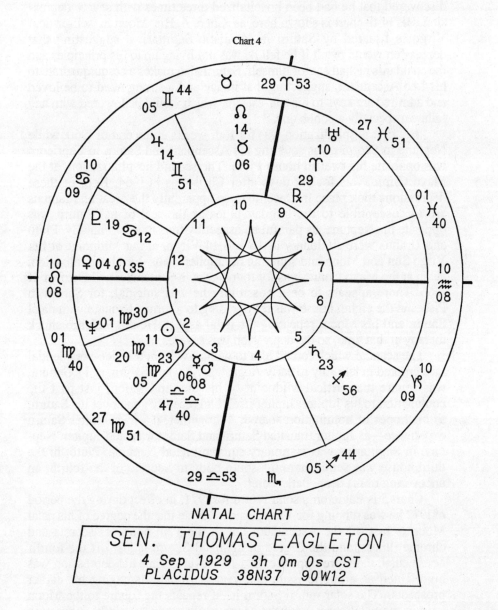

NATAL CHART

SEN. THOMAS EAGLETON
4 Sep 1929 3h 0m 0s CST
PLACIDUS 38N37 90W12

discovered that he had been hospitalized three times with severe depression. His birth chart is shown here as Chart 4. His Moon in self-critical Virgo is squared by Saturn in idealistic Sagittarius, suggesting that depression would result if he felt he was not living up to his principles and the standards he had set for himself. Saturn also makes a sesquiquadrate to his Leo Ascendant, suggesting that image and a strong need to be loved and admired are keys to his self-esteem, which would be lowered with any failure, especially a public one.

His first hospitalization was for four weeks at the end of 1960, while Neptune in Scorpio was squaring his Ascendant and Saturn in Capricorn was opposite his twelfth house Pluto. The second hospitalization, at the Mayo Clinic, was for six days after Christmas in 1964. Both of these depressions took place in December, so apparently the great and famous are as susceptible to the holiday blues as the rest of us. Saturn was opposite his Neptune, as painful an aspect by transit as it is natally. Pluto and Uranus were stationary at 16 and 14 Virgo, at the Midpoint of his Virgo Sun and Moon and squaring his Jupiter. His third hospitalization, again at the Mayo Clinic, was for four weeks in September and October of 1966. There appears to be a possibility he was suicidal, for Saturn in Pisces in the eighth house was retrograding to a form a t-square with natal Saturn and his Moon, repeating the natal aspect. He did undergo shock therapy at that time, so the depression was severe.

The scandal which forced him to withdraw from the vice-presidential race erupted in late July to early August, 1972, when Saturn, at 17 Gemini, was square that critical Midpoint of his Sun and Moon, just past the conjunction to his Jupiter. Jupiter itself had recently gone over his Saturn, as his hopes of nomination soared. Altogether, it was a Jupiter Saturn experience—as Jupiter transited Saturn and Saturn transited Jupiter. Neptune in Sagittarius was stationary squaring natal Neptune. Pluto, in the third house was semisquare his south node in Scorpio in the fourth, an uncovering of his deep, dark secret.

Chart 5 is Eagleton's solar return for 1971, in effect during the period of 1972 he was running for Vice President. Note that the degree of his natal Moon is just off the Ascendant, but in the 12th house of secrets and chronic illness, and the degree of his natal Saturn is just off the fourth house cusp, therefore opposite the Midheaven. Thus his depression was highlighted as a public issue that year, seriously damaging his career prospects. The solar return Saturn itself repeats the square to the Moon seen in the natal chart, with the Moon in Pisces in the sixth, suggesting emotional illness, and Saturn in the ninth house of politics. When a natal aspect is important, repetitions in the sky seem to bring up the issue again. (For instance, when Mars and Saturn form an aspect in the sky, I seem to have a rush of clients with that combination in their charts.) The solar

Chart 5

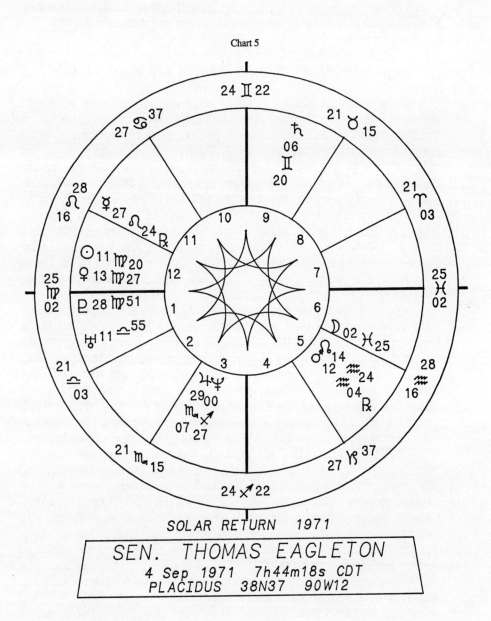

SOLAR RETURN 1971

SEN. THOMAS EAGLETON
4 Sep 1971 7h44m18s CDT
PLACIDUS 38N37 90W12

return Moon in Pisces is opposed by natal Neptune in the solar return twelfth, again emphasizing the senator's illness and the secret about it.

Depression Under Saturn Transits and Natal Aspects

Many people get the blues when transiting Saturn forms a difficult connection with key planets in their birth chart. Just as many use Saturn transits as spurs to realistic accomplishments, putting to work that popular Saturnian saying, " When the going gets tough, the tough get going." Yet many of these people also go through temporary slumps while they take in the lessons of Saturn. Why do Saturn transits bring them on? How can you consciously use them for your benefit? The blues are possibly due to facing up to reality, but they can also represent an overdose of Saturn's perfectionism and high ambitions. Remembering that depression itself is a healing process, the readings for each transit will give you clues to the process it represents. The issue will come up several times in the six to nine months a Saturn aspect is in effect, with direct and retrograde motions, and each time, you will get closer to resolution.

Although the readings are pitched toward transiting aspects, people with these aspects in their natal charts can also learn something about healing themselves. Here the challenge is harder, a mountain rather than a molehill. The difficulties are recurrent, especially during Saturn's aspects to its natal position at approximately 7, 14, 21, 28, and so on. To get more understanding of places where things went wrong, think about things that may have happened to you at those ages that may be underneath your feelings of sadness and negativity. You may need to go back and do some healing work about those eras and events that occurred during them.

SATURN TRANSITS TO THE SUN can be a blow to the inflated ego, as they force you to put up or shut up. After mourning the idealized self, however, you begin to mobilize your true core strengths and work on expressing your capabilities. SATURN TO THE MOON can mean serious depression, often as the result of a separation from someone you depended on or of the pressure to grow up. Sometimes the mother is getting older, or less available, or you confront the reality of who she or some other significant female figure is, as opposed to your fantasies. As this transit progresses, you wipe away your tears and get on with the business of establishing some security for yourself. SATURN TO MERCURY shows you obsessing on worries or sad thoughts or makes you confront your intellectual limitations. Saturn remedies would be working out a concrete plan and learning the new skills you need, maybe finally getting that piece of paper. Breathing exercises or aerobic exercise would alleviate depression with this transit, or with natal aspects between

Mercury and Saturn, including Saturn in Gemini, since some inhibition about breathing is indicated.

With SATURN TRANSITS TO VENUS, you confront the depressing realities of your love life, and may find love grown cold. Often, the sadder but wiser person decides to let go of fantasies about finding the ideal mate and gets practical. Surprisingly often people do make durable commitments under this transit. SATURN ASPECTS TO MARS personify the teaching that depression is anger turned inward. Often, there are realistic reasons why the expression of anger is blocked, for instance, that your opponent has you outclassed or controls your paycheck. The remedy is to channel and discipline your anger, using it to confront and deal with some major barrier to your goals.

When SATURN TRANSITS JUPITER, you may pay the price for excesses and unwise risk taking, and you have to learn the realistic limits to your expansiveness. Needless to say, this is sobering, yet after the sadness passes, you are wiser, not so prone to self-defeating excess. SATURN ASPECTS TO NATAL SATURN are phases of the Saturn cycle, repeating all natal aspects to Saturn and making you come to terms once more with those lifelong issues. The pain as you confront those realities can still motivate you to work on your barriers.

SATURN ASPECTS TO URANUS make you play hardball with the establishment, as you confront how it restricts or disapproves of your contrariety. Often, after you've gotten over being angry or depressed, you get practical and work on a compromise of some sort that lets you express your personal genius within the establishment. How difficult that is depends on how much of a Uranian hardhead you are. SATURN TRANSITS TO NEPTUNE are very depressing and often lead to the POOR MEs, as you tap into that Neptunian feeling of helplessness and victimization. It's a rude awakening, a shouting match between fantasy and reality. You may wallow in self-pity as you say goodbye to certain cherished illusions or addictions, but you ultimately reassess what parts of your visions can be brought down to earth, and you get to work on them.

When SATURN MAKES AN ANGLE TO PLUTO, a very serious confrontation with the powers that be can ensue, and you can hit a stone wall in dealing with them or in confronting your own Plutonian personality traits. Extreme remedies like rolfing or a period of withdrawal and hard work on your own barriers may be required to make any headway against these calcified patterns. The depression here is grief, often long-suppressed grief, and the mourning in itself is a powerful healing.

SATURN ASPECTS TO THE ASCENDANT may be depressing in terms of coming to terms with your appearance or physical limitations, with aging as an issue—even for 24 year olds. Yet, they spur you to be more disciplined about taking care of yourself and may give you the strength to diet, do yoga, or engage in some other structured regimen. At the same time, these can be read as SATURN ASPECTS TO THE ASCENDANT/DESCENDANT AXIS, which may bring sadness about your presentation of yourself to the world and the limitations in your relationships which result from it. You learn to be more responsible for the way you present yourself and more courageous in putting your capabilities forward. You also learn not to take so much responsibility for others, even though they may play games or withdraw for a period of time to try to get you to take care of them again.

SATURN ASPECTS TO THE MC/IC AXIS present opportunities to grow out of dependency into more capability, so they may very well bring more success, as well as more responsibility. There can be growing pains, as well as all the dynamics given under the letdown phenomenon. Growing up and leaving your roots behind can be very sad, and there may be actual aging or debilitation on the part of parental figures to be somber about. This, however, is often a time of achievement, of reaping what you've sown.

Getting at the Roots of Your Own Depression

If you are seriously depressed, ask yourself the following questions to understand more about where it's coming from. Chances are, with any Saturn problem, you know quite specifically WHAT you're upset about, but these questions can help you isolate and correct the underlying beliefs and attitudes. Each is keyed to a house in the Capricorn Rising wheel. Thus the first question relates to Capricorn on the first house, the second question to Aquarius on the second, and so on.

What pressure am I putting on myself to have a facade of perfection or to always look fully capable?

What have I lost that I value? Am I allowing myself to mourn that loss or do I believe I have to be cool and detached about it?

How did a false belief that I had to be somehow saintly or self-sacrificing enter into the problem? Am I using drugs, alcohol, or food to block my feelings of sadness and thus delay the healing process?

What am I angry at, underneath it all? What do I think would happen if I allowed this anger to come to the surface?

Do I stubbornly insist on tackling this problem in the same old way, or can

I come up with some creative solutions?

Am I working obsessively and thus adding to the depression by mental fatigue?

In what way have I been excessively dependent on relationships and thus refused to grow up? Is the pressure to grow up part of my feeling of loss at this time?

Is wounded pride part of the problem? How was that a false pride, rather than a realistic feeling of self-worth?

Which former beliefs and attitudes that governed my behavior in this kind of situation failed me? Can I take a practical look at what went wrong?

Am I excessively concerned with my public image? Do I want everyone to love me always, and is my feeling of loss related to this need for unconditional love?

Do I feel betrayed or manipulated by my former friends or support systems? Did they somehow resent or undercut my success?

Does my sorrow come from facing a truth I formerly hid from? How can facing the truth help me to avoid such difficulties in the future?

Writing or thinking about these questions should help you begin to tackle the underpinnings of the slump you are in. By identifying its roots, you can begin to get a clearer idea of what to do to help yourself.

Astrological Cues to Relieving Depression

In keeping with the homeopathic principle of like curing like, we can derive hints on how to relieve a depression or speed up the process by using the same Capricorn Rising wheel that helped us understand its origins. Understand that these suggestions and all the remedies given in this chapter are not intended to replace health care and psychotherapeutic treatment for the seriously depressed person who needs it.

Capricorn on the first house suggests some physical discipline, such as yoga or a restricted diet, can help. Aquarius on the second calls for reassessing your values and coming to see the loss from a new perspective. Be willing to experiment. Detach from material things as an indicator of your worth.

Pisces on the third, which was so meaningful in terms of understanding the roots of this emotional illness, also has much to offer in its alleviation. Look for the spiritual meaning of this painful situation. Prayer and meditation are powerful, as well as writing out the things that are bothering you. In moderation, escape IS helpful, especially such gentle Neptunian escapes as listening to music, going to the movies, or visiting the seashore. Fantasy, also, can be a consolation, if used in moderation, and can help you come up with a new vision to work toward.

Aries on the fourth house showed that the roots of depression are frequently found in anger. To stop turning the anger inward, recognize that anger may be underlying your depression, and dig down into the roots of it.. Come to feel at home with your anger. It doesn't matter if it's "justified" or "unjustified," it's still real to you. Take action to change your situation. Physical exertion, such as running regularly, has proven to be helpful in lifting depression.

With Taurus on the fifth house, learn the value of a hobby or some form of creative outlet. This will ground you and give you some peace. Working with natural materials or simply being out in nature can be comforting, as a reminder that life is abundance, not limitation.

Gemini on the sixth shows the power of the mind in both creating and relieving depression. Find the humor in your situation, no matter how black. Explore the mental source of your psychosomatic ailments. Pay attention to your thoughts and notice how negative ones can limit you. When not engaged in compulsively, work can be therapy, taking your mind off your troubles.

Cancer on the seventh points out the need to find some nurturing relationships—or discover the joys of nurturing others. You need to feel needed just now. Renew family ties, if they are comforting.

With Leo on the eighth, play is restorative, so let the child part of you come out. Even if you're not happy, act as if you were, and you'll find a surprising lift in your mood.

The strength of Virgo on the ninth is that when you're depressed about a failure, analyze what additional knowledge or skills are needed and get to work acquiring them. It's time, also, to take a critical look at former belief systems and attitudes that may be getting you down, especially the belief you must be perfect.

Libra on the tenth house shows that stimulating the depression is a place where you choose not to make more choices, so decide to let it be all right that you are undecided. Cultivate a balanced attitude about your goals rather than expect to be perfect at them. Know also that you cannot please the whole world and get everyone to love you.

Scorpio on the eleventh house suggests the helpfulness of a support group or even group therapy.

With Sagittarius on the twelfth house, take in new spiritual or philosophical perspectives. Use positive thinking to eliminate self-defeating patterns, especially visualizations. It would also be helpful to study the unconscious seriously, such as taking a psychology course.

Put your own chart into the Capricorn Rising wheel, with the degree of your natal Saturn on the cusp, and your natal planets in the corresponding equal house cusp divisions. This would show reasons why you tend to get depressed. Pay special attention to the house where natal Saturn falls; it might show childhood losses that predispose you to depression. It would also indicate the area where perfectionism arises, making you depressed when you fall short of unrealistic standards. The house where transiting Saturn falls or where it aspects natal planets may also give you clues to a current case of the blues.

Flower Essences for Depression and Discouragement

The Bach remedies themselves were developed during the Depression era of the early 1930s. They reflect the climate of their time, in which these three emotions were so prevalent—fear, discouragement, and depression. Thus the Bach remedies reveal a whole spectrum of kinds of depression. It is important not to overload yourself with Saturn remedies. When I first started using them, I combined every single one of the remedies for depression and discouragement in one bottle, never wanting to suffer from depression again. With this "kill or cure" move, I went through one of the worst depressions ever, in a healing crisis that was unnecessarily rough.

Those who need the remedy ELM are capable people yet often feel inadequate and are overwhelmed at times by responsibilities. GENTIAN is for feelings of discouragement and resultant self-doubt and depression. It is useful for the kind of person with a negative outlook, who gets discouraged easily and quits. GORSE alleviates despair and hopelessness and the feeling of utter despondency after the failure of many attempts. It is good for the chronically ill or those who have struggled a long time with a problem. LARCH is useful for the person who expects to fail, so fails to make the attempt. It is also good if you are feeling inferior and despondent due to lack of self-confidence. MUSTARD appears to be for depression that is biochemical, the type of dark depression which descends for no known cause and can lift just as suddenly.

A number of the more modern essences may be useful for depression and discouragement as well. BORAGE is excellent if you are feeling disheartened and discouraged, as it brings you cheerful courage and confidence in facing danger. SCOTCH BROOM helps motivation and perseverance, gives faith to those who are in despair, and stops pessimism. PENSTEMON gives inner strength when you are overwhelmed by challenges and self-doubt. BLACKBERRY strengthens those who direct their thoughts to limitation and lack and is known to help conscious manifestation of goals. PENNYROYAL is useful against negative thoughts and thought forms, and keeps you from absorbing negativity from others. It encourages hard workers to rest, and calms obsessions.

Using the Saturn Chant and Rosaries

The Saturn chant is especially useful in getting to the root of depression and mobilizing you. Do not forget, however, to do all the crying that you must in order to resolve the sorrow. The crying may come up as you use the Saturn chant, especially with a rosary, and also in using some of the flower essences. Our culture makes us want to cut off our feelings and escape from them, yet it is that very attempt to escape that creates and prolongs depression.

The Saturn chant is as follows:

DAH TI KAH
DAH TI KAH
DAH IT KAH
OH AY

Do the Saturn chant, repeating it slower and slower. Picture an open space between the sounds, like a TV screen, and let images appear which will tell you more of what you need to help yourself. You are stimulating healing for the roots of the depression. The Saturn rosaries, given in the table on the opposite page, are good for working through sorrow and feelings of blockage and frustration, correlating with specific aspects in your chart or with Saturn transits.

Saturn Rosaries for Depression

ASPECT:	BEAD PATTERN:	CHANT:	SOURCE OF DEPRESSION:
SATURN/	RED	OH HAY YAH	Self-doubt, deflation
SUN	RED	OH HAY YAH	of the ego, feeling
	BROWN	DAH TI KAH	inadequate to the
			challenges now

operating.

SATURN/	WHITE	SI IDRIAH	Loss of someone
MOON	WHITE	SI IDRIAH	depended on; Being
	BROWN	DAH TI KAH	forced to be more
			independent.

SATURN/	PURPLE	OH HI TI NAH	Seeing reality clearly;
MERCURY	PURPLE	OH HI TI NAH	confronting
	BROWN	DAH TI KAH	intellectual lacks or
			deficits.

SATURN/	GREEN	NAH TI NAH	Sorrow over loss of
VENUS	GREEN	NAH TI NAH	love or lack of it.
	BROWN	DAH TI KAH	Demoralized about
			one's attractiveness.

SATURN/	BLACK	NAY ZI DAY HOH HI MAH	Held-in anger at authority,
MARS	BLACK	NAY ZI DAY HOH HI MAH	being blocked in achieving desires.
	BROWN	DAH TI KAH	Feeling like a loser.

SATURN/	YELLOW	HI SU MAI YOH	Loss of formerly boundless hopes,
JUPITER	YELLOW	HI SU MA YOH	confronting the limits of expansiveness.
	BROWN	DAH TI KAH	

SATURN/	BROWN	DAH TI KAH	Pressure to conform;
URANUS	BROWN	DAH TI KAH	necessity to fit in so
	SILVER	NAH MITRIAH	goals can be reached.

SATURN/	BROWN	DAH TI KAH	Facing up to reality,
NEPTUNE	BROWN	DAH TI KAH	giving up fantasies or
	MINT	OH MYS	illusions. Reaching the
			depths of depression.

SATURN/	BROWN	DAH TI KAH	Deep and sometimes
PLUTO	BROWN	DAH TI KAH	long-suppressed
	NATURAL	TI OH	mourning.

A Bibliography of Helpful Books on Depression

DeRosis, Helen A., MD., and Victoria Y. Pelligrino. *The Book of Hope: How Women Can Overcome Depression*. New York: Bantam, 1977.

This excellent self-help book not only traces the roots of depression in women's lives but also gives specific techniques for getting out of it. DeRosis was born 4/12/18 in Freeport, New York.

Dufty, William. *Sugar Blues*. New York: Warner Books, 1976.

Sugar's alarming multiple effects on mind and body, including its addictive properties. Our culture's part in creating a dependency on it through advertising and putting it in foods.

Flach, Frederic, MD. *The Secret Strength of Depression*. Revised Edition New York: Bantam Books , 1986.

Although a strong believer in antidepressants, this psychiatrist has many valuable insights into the roots of depression and ways of relieving it.

Scarf, Maggie. *Unfinished Business: Pressure Points in the Lives of Women*. New York: Doubleday, 1980.

Excellent insights into the reasons women suffer more depression than men and the various life stages when we are more prone to it.

1 Lois Rodden, *Astro-Data II* (San Diego,Ca: ASC), 1980.
2 Elvis was born 1/8/35 at 4:45 a.m. CST in Tupelo, Miss, 88W43, 34N16, according to Lois Rodden's *Astro Data II*.
3 This data was taken from Lois Rodden's *Astro Data II*, ACS, San Diego, CA, 1980.
4 Ibid.

CHAPTER SIX

EYEBALL TO EYEBALL WITH URANUS:
A CELEBRITY INTERVIEW

Knowing what I do about the essence of Uranus, it seemed presumptuous—and very possibly even dangerous—for me to speak for Uranus. I mean, I've got some transits coming up that don't bear thinking about! Why tempt fate? I decided to interview him and let him speak for himself. It was a little hard to hear, because we met in a disco, and it was hard to read him, behind those dark glasses, spikey punk hair and black leather jacket. To tell you the truth, I wasn't even sure it was a male—it was one of those androgynous types. But let me report what he said, occasionally edited for the sake of propriety, as he was really heavy into four-letter words.

DC: I'm really thrilled to be talking to you. I've always considered you an exciting astrological and astronomical personage.

UR: Cut the crap! You're scared to death of me. They all are.

DC: You're right about that. I guess with you nobody gets away with hypocrisy. But sometimes the scariest people are the most exciting. You and your Uranian followers really shake people up, so there's always something going on when you're around. The Aquarians, for instance. The main thing I notice about Aquarians is that they're so different from most people.

UR: What's the meanest thing you can say to an Aquarian? "You Aquarians are all alike!" Aquarians and Uranians like to think of themselves as very special and unprecedented. In fact, each of them would like a trophy inscribed, "World's Most Unique Individual." You could mass market those trophies. If you tell Aquarians they're not so different, they think there's something wrong with your intelligence. The truth is, each person is unique. There are no two people exactly alike, just as there are no two snowflakes the same. And yet, like the snowflakes, you can blend into the snowfall, and become one of the masses. Thus, paradoxically, Uranus is about uniqueness and it's about mass movements and popular trends.

DC: Uranus is also said to have much to do with our identity. How does that connection arise?

UR: The thing which is different about us, which causes us to stand out in some way, shapes the way we see ourselves and the labels others give us. It strikes me that much of what people base their identity on is not Uranus but Saturn. It's what they've been in the past, especially the trappings of roles or status. Then a Uranus transit comes along and forces them to challenge and change that identity, often because that role or status is lost. Saturn particularly shows the ways people limit themselves, and they often define themselves in terms of what they can and cannot do. But under Uranus transits, folks get tired of the old limits, stretching themselves to experiment, and thus their identity has to stretch to meet new abilities and circumstances. There is a need to change the self-concept periodically, because people evolve over the years, and the self-concept doesn't usually keep pace with the evolution.

In fact, for most people, identity is fixed in the teen years, based on whether they were popular or not, whether they did well in school or not, whether they lived on the wrong side of the tracks, whether they were good in sports. As adults, people still tend to think of themselves as that klutz or that unpopular, pimply person. They have the Saturnian tendency to crystallize into a particular mold and to take on a self-concept based on the limits accepted as theirs in that teenage period. Under Uranus transits, they question and break out of those strictures. As you can see, the question of "identity" is a complex one, and often quite artificial, not based on your true self, which is the Sun.

DC: Recently, I've been questioning why appearance has anything to do with identity. Appearance is a function of the Ascendant and fairly superficial, while the real self is the Sun.

UR: Appearance has to do with separateness. A primary task for teens is to establish separateness. Uranian people often dress or act in ways that cause them to be even more at odds with society, in order to establish their identity. Teenagers are Uranian and make a point of shocking their elders with their dress.

I'd have to concede that appearance does fall under the heading of Uranus, but only because society has so much difficulty accepting anyone who looks different. If you didn't have such a fetish about appearance, Uranians would have to find some other way of showing their separateness. Even the symbol for Aquarius suggests separation as an issue.

The schism or break between the two halves of the symbol suggests the boundary between self and other.

DC: Speaking of separateness, it's a strange thing. Aquarians are always surrounded by people, and yet I find a kind of loneliness about them too.

UR: Loneliness can come from being unique which begins to explain another paradox—the fact that Uranus, which is all about individuality, also rules groups. The loneliness of being different is assuaged by finding groups of like-minded individuals. "Sure I'm different," the Uranian says, "but look at all the others like me." Thus teens cling fiercely to their peer group, radicals swear allegiance to their comrades in the cause. Within that group, however, the structures, the roles, the pressure to conform are intense. You can only be different if you're just like the rest. Dependency on the group gives them security to withstand society's pressures.

DC: Aquarians are such rebels! Why is that?

UR: Aquarians and Uranians are known for their rebelliousness, but Uranians don't necessarily start out being rebellious...they only start out being different. Once seen as different, however, they're pressured to be the same as everyone else, to fit into the mold. The Aquarius Rising wheel has Scorpio on the tenth house, showing the repressive reaction of authority figures to the Uranian person—and the resentful response of Uranians, who would do themselves in to spite authority. The kind of person who becomes the die-hard rebel—the radical, the biker—does so because differentness gets crystallized into rebellion and defiance. The more Uranians break rank, the more coercion they experience, and the more defiant they become.

People with a strong Uranus are greatly feared by the parts of society that want to keep things the way they are. Uranian people propel society into change, leading the way with trends that the rest of you belatedly follow, once the shock value has worn off. Even while adopting their clothing, their music, their pastimes, and more slowly, their life styles, society labels such people "weirdos," "kooks," and "radicals," and often doles out heavy penalties for being different.

Uranians are distinguished, by and large, by society's disapproval of them. Yet who is to say who best serves the whole and what is the most evolved way to serve? Uranians serve by shaking the rest of humanity out of complacency, pushing them to change what is. Surely bikers do that as effectively as anti-nuclear demonstrators do. Teenagers, too, put in years of service as shakers. They secretly bring social change into your houses, Trojan horse fashion, in the form of their music, their media, and their mores.

Yet everyone has Uranus in their chart, so every person has the need to be an individual in their own right, to change, and to break away from the past. Instead of disowning that part of themselves and ostracizing the people who dare to act out this need they all have, it would be healthier for individuals and for society to make allowances for expressing individuality in a balanced and constructive way.

DC: You're not always so concerned about doing things in a balanced and constructive way. I hear you're responsible for atomic energy—for things like Hiroshima. Look at the chart for the bomb explosion. You're right up at the top. (See Chart 6.)

UR: Oh, yeah, and you remember the Chernobyl nuclear accident? I was right up there at the top of the chart for that gig too. I had a little help from my buddy Pluto. (See Chart 7.) But you see, the world has changed radically as a result of nuclear power. It has the capacity to destroy you, it is true, but that very fact is in the end the thing that will unite you into one world. Another paradox.

DC: Looking ahead a bit, what do you anticipate it will be like when you move in with Capricorn?

UR: I'm not looking forward to it at all, because that dude wants to cramp my style. Like, you know, discipline and limits and all that horse pucky. That's okay. He'll get more than he bargained for with me as a tenant. I'll be the best thing that's happened to that old grouch in a long time, after everything stops rocking and shaking. Some of his entourage—his corporate monkey suit types—are gonna shock him with the things I put them up to doing.

DC: So you expect to bring some conservatives around to your way of thinking?

UR: I've got a lot of right wingers in my cadre already, although they don't know they're serving my purposes. They like to think they're free agents, but they're so conservative, they're radical. To give you an example, did you ever take a look at Anita Bryant's chart? She's got me up on her MC, along with Venus and Mars. Kind of makes you wonder, doesn't it, what she actually gets off on? I was in Taurus in those days, though. Talk about conservative! (See Chart 8.)

Chart 6

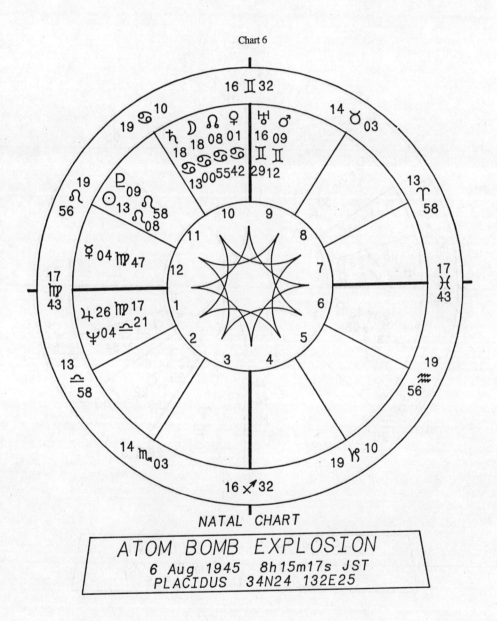

NATAL CHART

ATOM BOMB EXPLOSION
6 Aug 1945   8h15m17s JST
PLACIDUS   34N24 132E25

Chart 7

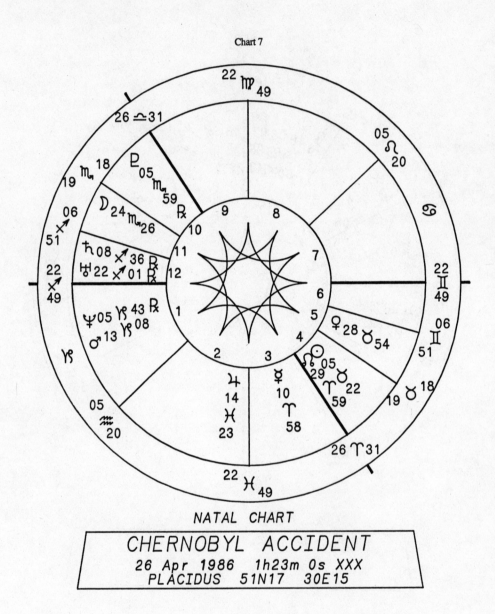

NATAL CHART

CHERNOBYL ACCIDENT
26 Apr 1986   1h23m 0s XXX
PLACIDUS   51N17   30E15

Chart 8

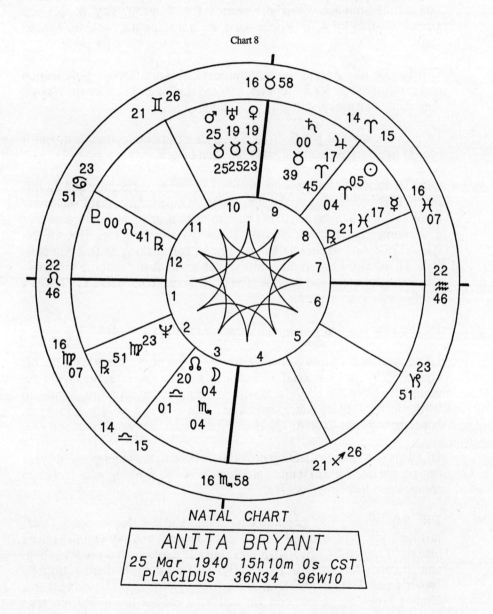

NATAL CHART

ANITA BRYANT
25 Mar 1940 15h10m 0s CST
PLACIDUS 36N34 96W10

DC: I'm surprised you'd associate with folks like her. I wouldn't think you could stomach what she stands for. I mean, gay people are Uranians—they're your people—and she's leading the backlash against them.

UR: People like Anita serve my purposes. I work through polarization and create dissent. Shake 'em up, get 'em thinking. I don't care WHAT they think, you see, just that they DO think.

DC: That's a weird perspective. So...I don't know, so detached. But it sounds like you like some signs better than others.

UR: Get stuffed! All signs are equal! I just work differently and on different things depending on the sign. I cannot hide the fact that I was pretty comfortable in Sagittarius, didn't have to work nearly so hard because he's a thinking sign himself and he loves his freedom too. But OPINIONATED! And so sure he's right! I had a ball shaking up that pompous jerk. Then, too, I got to take potshots at some of my favorite targets—religion, education, and the law. The orthodoxy. HOOOOOEY! I haven't had this much fun in years!

DC: So how is it that you work differently in different signs?

UR: I work a lot through the elements. Through the ideas with the air signs, with the emotional resistances for the water signs, with the materializations for earth, and with startling actions for fire. Some are harder for me—those water signs would like to drown me. It's a dirty job, but somebody has to do it. Otherwise the human race would mummify.

DC: This is a book on healing problems related to the outer planets. What can people do to heal Uranian problems? We're working with tools like rosaries and flower essences.

UR: Say beads? You've got to be joking! And that flower essence stuff just isn't scientific enough for me. But how dare you say Uranians need healing! They're all VERRRRRY evolved. It's society that needs healing, and Uranians can see it all too clearly. That's what gets them in trouble. But it's not THEIR problem, it's society's problem. If you've got a Uranus problem, go out and get active to change the world. Protest! Demonstrate! What about you? What are you doing for the collective good?

DC: I'm an astrologer. I see astrology as an agent for change.

UR: Yeah? What do you put on the line? Just sitting there with a dumb circle and all these hen scratches on it?

DC: Well, it's an alternative life style. We don't get much respect from the establishment and none of us is are making a fortune off it. People ridicule us.

UR: Yeah, well, if enough people call you a donkey, maybe you ought to get a saddle. If you lead an alternate life style, it's a hell of a tame one. The bikers, now, I really like them. They put everything on the line for their beliefs, and, hoo boy, do they shake people up! Oh, yeah, they're my people!

DC: But astrology shakes people up, too, and increases their consciousness.

UR: I'll grant you astrology was a shocker in the Sixties. It was a rocket booster to consciousness for the masses in those days, when I was hanging out with Pluto. But it's pretty ho hum now. Everybody has done it to death.

DC: Oh, no, I still get a virgin now and then, and that first chart reading really blows their minds.

UR: You're all too comfortable in it now. National conferences of astrologers, organizations, certifications, and curriculums. Next thing you know there'll be licenses. I mean, LICENSES! What does that have to do with me?

DC: But we've got to have standards!

UR: NAH, it's bull shit. You need to go out on a limb, take a risk, forge new territory, make a statement.

DC: I'm not ready for that. I'm pretty comfortable where I am. One further question. I know it's a long way off and the future depends on what happens now—free will and all that. But, can you give us any idea what to expect with Uranus in Aquarius?

UR: I don't want to say too much about it because the kinds of changes I work for depend a lot on shock value. I will say this—it'll give you a sneak preview of what to expect from the Age of Aquarius.

DC: Oh, yes, we're all looking forward to that. Aren't you proud to have an age all your own?

UR: Harumph. Well, I couldn't have done it alone. But all those windbag spiritual folks who're looking forward to it will get some surprises. They think it's going to be heaven. We'll all live in PEEEAAAACCCCEE. Peace? Harmony? That's a die-hard Age of Pisces pipe dream. I've never been about peace. Me? Uranus? Give me a break! Yo! I've gotta split! See ya.

DC: I hope not. At least not too soon. Forge new territory, make a statement.

1 Lois Rodden, *Profiles of Women*. (Tempe, AZ: AFA, 1979), p.21.

CHAPTER SEVEN

THE ADOLESCENT, THE PERPETUAL ADOLESCENT, AND THE 40-YEAR-OLD [1]

What do the adolescent, the perpetual adolescent, and the forty-year-old have in common? Their psychology, as we will see, has many similarities. They share many of the dynamics of the planet Uranus, in that they are struggling to find their identity and individuality, to establish their place in the world. This is done in a manner that puts them at odds with society. They challenge and often outrage society's expectations and refuse to conform. In fact, their single most distinguishing characteristic is our disapproval of them.

Their charts are also very much keyed into the planet Uranus, temporarily in the case of the teenager and the 40-year-old, permanently in the case of the perpetual adolescent. In this chapter, the Aquarius Rising wheel will deepen our understanding of teenagers and 40-year-olds. For insights into the perpetual adolescent, we will look at the charts of some bikers.

The Purpose of Adolescence

Is adolescence just a trying time to live through—a mine field for teens and their parents to cross gingerly? Or, is it a productive phase of life? Studying human development, we learn that adolescence is a crucial and positive process. The young person is struggling to gain a separate identity and let go of child-like dependency. Granted, the process is hard, filled with emotional upheavals and rebelliousness. But if parents and teens understand what is going on and communicate, it can be easier on everyone.

Astrologers believe Uranus governs adolescence. Yet, Uranus is a permanent part of our chart and is active by transit throughout our lives. Teens are not a race apart—the struggle for identity and independence is life-long. Adults who see teens as vastly different have repressed the painful struggle they passed through on the way to becoming adults. To explore adolescence, I chose the Aquarius Rising wheel, since Uranus and its sign, Aquarius, are most closely related to this period. I set up a chart with Aquarius on the first house and the other signs following in order around the houses. As you will see from the descriptions, this tool gives many valuable insights. It also gives insights into Uranian periods of life, like age forty, the newly divorced, or other times of sudden, unexpected change. Take the readings, delete the references to adolescence, and you will have a picture of the psychology of people of any age going through such a period of upheaval.

AQUARIUS ON THE FIRST HOUSE: The first house is the outer shell of the self, including the physical appearance, dress, mannerisms, and the front we put on to deal with the world. Teenagers' dress and appearance are faddish and modern like Aquarius, changing styles frequently to be fresh and different and to separate themselves clearly from the adult world, shockingly so at times. That, of course, is the purpose—to demonstrate that they are separate and different. If styles change often, so too do young people's identities, trying on this role and that to find one that truly suits.

Aquarius is the sign of the group, and on the first house, it shows the importance of the gang or crowd. Teens want foremost to belong, so their dress, appearance, and slang conform to what is "in" at the moment. Being friendly and "cool" are Aquarian. Teens aspire to coolness almost desperately, pretending nothing bothers them, when in reality, adolescence is a period of painful turmoil.

PISCES ON THE SECOND HOUSE: The second house represents money and those things we value—tangible and intangible. The sign Pisces here shows teens are confused about values, shifting from one to another as emotions are played on and played out. Pisces people are idealistic, especially in regard to money, which is common among teenagers. Dreams of riches and glory alternate with sympathy for the unfortunate.

Realism about earning and using money is rare at this age—parents complain that kids think it grows on trees. This is understandable, since few teens have practical experience in earning and managing their own funds. They are becoming more conscious of money and the magic it seems to work, while still operating from the childhood perception that money magically appears whenever parents see fit to bestow it. Small wonder, then, that at this stage, money is a mystical, magical substance that comes and goes in mysterious ways. With practical experience, for most of us, money becomes more real, but many of us retain some adolescent fantasies about money.

ARIES ON THE THIRD HOUSE: The third house represents thinking, communication, and near relatives. Aries is extremely competitive, and competition is very much a part of adolescents' way of thinking. Sports are popular in high school—whether participating or rooting—and the football hero is a much bigger deal than the honor student. Teens are already absorbing adults' status-seeking, and knowing where you stand in relation to others is also part of establishing your identity. Unfortunately, their ranking devices (cheerleader, prom queen, student body president) don't have much to do with success in the real world. Yet "failure" in these areas may leave a poor self-concept that remains throughout life. Parents can help by supporting and praising their offspring's talents and creating opportunities for them to pursue their abilities.

Communication patterns among teenage groups can also be Arien— competitive ("ranking"), direct, and often aggressive. Talking tough and macho covers up fears and insecurities. It may also give them courage to face scary new adult tasks, for "acting as if" can get them through new situations with self-confidence.

The third house also shows relationships with brothers, sisters, and near relatives. Here Aries' competitiveness shows up in the intense sibling rivalry we so often see at this stage—arguments, verbal and physical attempts to dominate, and active hostility. Sometimes brothers and sisters are the safest competitors, sometimes they are simply in the way, and sometimes they catch displaced anger toward authority figures. Sibling rivalry can be intense, but it's generally just a phase.

TAURUS ON THE FOURTH HOUSE: The fourth house shows what gives us security and how we regard the nurturing function of our parents, usually our mothers. This placement is one of the pardoxes of Aquarius' rebelliousness. Taurus is warm and stable, but fairly conservative. Thus, even though they protest against parents' "old fashionedness," teens actually get a good deal of security from it. They need stability at home and derive peace of mind from traditions and routine. Even though they may not be home to enjoy it, they like knowing there's food on the table and a roof overhead.

While teens seem to change constantly (Aquarius on the first), they really don't want their home or their parents to change that much or even, if put to the test, for Mom and Dad to be modern. Parents who try to keep up with today's fashions and life-styles meet a surprising degree of resentment. Unwavering solidity at home gives teens something definite to rebel against in order to establish themselves as separate and different—a process teens must go through on their way to adulthood.

The fourth house also shows mother and how one regards her. Taurus is a warm, down-to-earth, earth-mother sign, and that's how teenagers basically look at mother. "She's not too smart, but she's always there when I need her." Taurus has to do with money, and of course, they believe you've got it if you could just be persuaded to part with it. If you find this description unflattering, wait 'til we get to the tenth house, which is how they feel about father!

GEMINI ON THE FIFTH HOUSE: The fifth house is love affairs, leisure time activities, children, and creativity. Gemini here shows that brothers and sisters are seen as "just children." Romances among teens are also Geminian in nature—fickle, ever-changing, and existing mainly in the head. Gemini is communication, and teens talk to or about their current love for hours on end, while your phone bill soars. But communication is one of the skills teen romances help develop—learning what the opposite sex is all about and how to talk to them. At the same time the love is a sounding board for finding out about themselves and learning to express their feelings. With self-expression a by-product of those heart-to-heart talks, do you really mind the phone bill so much? Too bad you cannot deduct it as tuition, because that's what it really is.

CANCER ON THE SIXTH HOUSE: The sixth house rules work and health. Work opportunities for teens are usually home, food, or family oriented, like the sign Cancer (baby-sitting, yard-work, fast food restaurants, or working in the family business). This is a crucial phase of development, allowing them security while they sort through their reactions to the world of work.

Many teen health problems seem related to conflicts over dependency, with weight gain and poor nutrition typical. The breasts and menses, ruled by the Moon, develop at this stage of life, bringing emotional and biological turbulence. Dependency also seems to be at the root of a major teen health problem—pregnancy. One in four sexually active girls becomes pregnant. In my years as a social worker in prenatal clinics, I found that teens did not get pregnant to become more independent. On the contrary, pregnancy bound them more closely to their mothers. Teenage mothers have more health problems and pregnancy complications. Drinking is another health problem, with one child in five becoming a problem drinker by grade 12. Here, alcohol abuse also seems related to conflicts over dependency and to attempts to cope with the emotional upheavals of adolescence, while retaining that cherished facade of Aquarian coolness.

LEO ON THE SEVENTH HOUSE: The seventh house shows our capacity for long-term, committed relationships, and Leo's main concern is the self. Most teens have not developed the capacity for commitment and sharing, so a majority of teenage marriages fail. Teens typically act as though the world revolves around them, and most are too narcissistic to give much to relationships. Rightfully so, in that the real commitment at this stage has to be to finding and developing oneself. Until they have a solid identity, a true and firm center, they cannot relate fully without being thrown off center.

VIRGO ON THE EIGHTH HOUSE: Birth, sex, and death are eighth house concerns. More teenagers are involved in premartial sex now than in the past, and parents need to be aware of this. The increasing amount of teenage sex aside, Virgo on this house says that most teens are not emotionally equipped to handle it. Virgo is an inhibited, virginal sign, not liberated about sex. More and more young people are feeling pressured into sex to feel part of the group. Engaging in sexuality before you are ready can be emotionally damaging. Naturally, maturity is an individual matter—one 16-year-old may be far more mature than another 18- or 19-year-old.

LIBRA ON THE NINTH HOUSE: The ninth house deals with higher education and one's philosophy of life. With Libra on the ninth, the major decision a teen may face is between college and marriage. Some, of course, view college as primarily a place to find a suitable mate. Marriage and the onset of a family may also interrupt education. Many teens believe that if they can just find the right mate, they will live happily ever after. Thus, they make another person God and look to that person to meet all their needs. Needless to say, it doesn't work. Libra on the ninth could also contribute to adolescent idealism, to the heart-felt belief in justice and fair play.

SCORPIO ON THE TENTH HOUSE: This highly meaningful house shows how we deal with authority figures, especially the father. Authority is an extremely important issue for teens to resolve, and they approach it with Scorpio's emotional intensity. They often view power as corrupt and controlling, while perceiving and resenting any discrepancy between what adults preach and what they do and their parents receive the closest scrutiny of all. Like the scorpion's sting, troubled teens do things out of spite to hurt their parents, but they themselves are harmed far more in the process. Any hint that you are trying to dominate will cause them to resist or strike back.

　　To give teens their due, parents and other adults can be much too authoritarian because they feel their authority being challenged and their power slipping away. A power struggle can set in, with neither side willing to give an inch. Yet, the key function of Scorpio is transformation, and the process of resisting parental authority is part and parcel of the adolescents' struggle to transform themselves from children to adults. If it is a bitter struggle, if it often feels like the scorpion's sting, this only indicates that the young person is having tremendous difficulty making that separation.

The tenth house also shows what the individual hopes to accomplish in life, and Scorpio there says a great deal about youthful idealism. The young person believes, with great intensity, that it is possible to transform the troubled world we live in. If it seems to them that this can only be accomplished by destroying the current system, that's Scorpionic too—death and rebirth—and shows why we tend to be more radical when we are young.

SAGITTARIUS ON THE ELEVENTH: The eleventh house shows our friends, our relationship to groups, and our hopes, dreams, and wishes. Sagittarius is an expansive, gregarious sign, wanting to learn and grow. Teens primarily learn from friends, who may be weak on details and exaggerate, but who still profess to know it all. Whatever the best friend says will be taken on faith.

Much growth, however, does come from the groups and organizations teens belong to. Even sports-related groups teach teamwork and other important life skills. As for the hopes of teenagers, if they are too optimistic and expansive, that's all to the good. We wouldn't get anywhere at all if we didn't aim high in the beginning.

CAPRICORN ON THE TWELFTH HOUSE: This house shows underlying motivations and secrets we keep hidden from ourselves and others, as well as self-destructive behavior. With Aquarius on the first, teens seem almost compelled to prove their individuality. But Capricorn on the twelfth shows that, underneath it all, teens are much more conservative than they would have us see and far more motivated by security needs. Their automatic rejection of established ways of doing things is a front, part of the fight to develop a separate identity, rather than the whole truth about what teenagers will ultimately become.

Self-destructive behavior is shown by the sign on the twelfth house. Capricorn here reiterates how self-destructively teens can deal with the issues of authority and responsibility. Some rebel against all authority, others comply to the exclusion of developing their individuality. Some evade responsibility, others take on far too much at an early age in their quest to become adults. Going to extremes in these matters is destructive; to master this phase of development successfully, a fine balance is needed.

Hopefully, this trip around the Aquarius Rising wheel has clarified some reasons for teens' often-puzzling behavior. Each of us, in our struggle to become mature adults, has passed through this phase. If we have forgotten, if we have come to think of teens as "them," then we have repressed that struggle because it was painful. If you deal with teenagers, you may wish to read further on the psychology of adolescence. As we will see, parents or teachers around 40 are also going through important Uranus transits, signifying that conflicts not resolved in adolescence have resurfaced and may add to the discomfort of being with teenagers.

To get a clearer understanding of a particular teen, analyzing the natal chart and transits to it can be helpful. The young person who has a strong Uranus may have an especially difficult time of it as a teenager. This would include those with Uranus in the first or tenth house, aspecting the Sun or Moon, forming numerous aspects, or in a dynamic configuration such as a t-square or grand cross. This signifies an individual who must establish independence and uniqueness at all costs. Generally, such people follow the path not well-trodden, and their life task often involves some unique contribution. If you are involved with young people like these, do your best to cherish their individuality and to set them free on their own path, which may be so unlike yours as to be alien.

The Perpetual Adolescent

This section is trouble. In searching for segments of the population to be designated as perpetually adolescent, I already know that any such segment will rise up in protest and say that their behavior is not that of an adolescent—they are making a social statement. Indeed, all Uranian types could be said to be making a social statement. Gay people are. Bikers are. Even those with punk hairstyles and dress are. All those who lead alternate life styles are.

In fact, each of us could be said to be making a social statement in the areas of life Uranus governs in our charts, unless we've been frightened into conformity. (These are the houses where Uranus and Aquarius are located and planets aspected by Uranus.) In those areas of life, we take exception to what society says we ought to be and undertake to subvert the norm by actions or inactions designed for shock value. We're idealistic, provocative, arrogant and, in short, thoroughly adolescent about the whole thing. It's not just that we're exercising freedom of choice, because if what we're espousing became fashionable, we'd do an abrupt about-face and espouse the opposite. Being markedly different in some area of life is a safety valve for individuality, keeping us from becoming conforming automatons.

People with Uranus in the first house make a social statement through their appearance; people with Uranus in the second by income and how it is disposed of; in the third, it is by patterns of speech and thought; in the fourth by the home environment or lack of it. When Uranus is in the fifth, the social statement is in romantic choices or gets acted out by what their children are covertly encouraged to become. In the sixth, it is by abrupt job changes, precipitated by distaste for conforming to rules. Or, if there is absolutely no other outlet, the statement may be made through accidents.

In the seventh, the marriage partner or lack there of makes the statement for us; in the eighth, we do it through unusual sexual proclivities or by running up huge debts; in the ninth, by radical politics, nontraditional religions, or by refusing to complete our education. In the tenth house, the statement is in the nature of a public announcement—no one can miss our defiance of authority figures and society's career expectations. In the eleventh, we do it in groups—or in our choice of friends. In the twelfth, it is a secret; we are closeted in our rebellion, and thus we trip over it constantly.

Now that I've almost slipped off the hook, will I go back on by saying that there are, after all, perpetual adolescents? Would anyone deny that there are? The last angry man; the rebel without a cause; the fad freak. There are those who cannot begin to find their own center, because they are automatically stuck with being oppositional. If you say turn left, they will turn right proudly and defiantly, smirking at your gaucheness in choosing the left—and they walk straight into the open manhole you were suggesting they turn left to avoid. Such people are usually bright enough (Uranus is never stupid) to find some social criticism in which to cloak their angry contrariness. Although it is passé to invoke Freud, I think I hear him out there muttering that Uranus causes anal fixations.

For a safe group to pick on, we will look at the bikers. Few, if any, of them will ever read this, and it's a splendid opportunity to publish my collection of biker's charts. I was at one point related by marriage to one of them, and it was even suggested that I write a thoroughly bitchy astrology advice column for *Easy Rider* under the pseudonym of Moon Mama. You have to admire the bikers, in a way. They do exactly as they please, flaunt social conventions, and nobody messes with them. It's social protest all right, not an effete, intellectual protest, but a gutsy, vital, macho one. AND, just like any other Uranian outgroup, there is an incredible pressure on members to conform to the rules of the group.

The charts of several bikers are printed here with permission. BELIEVE ME, with permission! As would seem suitable for such dyed-in-the-leather Uranians, I'll comment on their charts as a group, rather than in-depth as individuals. Although this is a limited sample, it does at least cover several clubs. My friend, astrologer John Ruskell, bravely risked life and limb attempting to get me a larger sample through charts of bikers in his area, but had little success in infiltrating the group, as they were convinced he was a narc. If you've ever met John, you'd know this was the height of paranoia, but bikers do not trust easily. No, as you will see from the charts, Pluto figures far too strongly for that. It is second only to Uranian and Aquarian highlights. Fire signs, Sagittarius in particular, are either Sun, Moon, or rising signs as well.

Chart 9 is of that most famous biker of all, Evel Knieval; at least he made a name for himself on a bike. He has Aquarius rising, with the Moon square his Uranus/south node conjunction. Sagittarius is there, with Venus in that sign on the Midheaven. Chart 10 is a Hell's Angel, who has a t-square with Uranus, an 11th house Mercury, and Jupiter. (Jupiter/Uranus people positively reek of Uranus, as Jupiter expands it and makes it all the more sure of its own rightness.) The Plutonian element consists of Scorpio rising and Saturn in Scorpio on the ascendant. Chart 11, a member of the Vargos gang, has the same Pluto/Uranus mix, with Sun, Venus, and Mercury conjunct in Scorpio trining Uranus. The Moon and Uranus are conjunct in Leo opposite Jupiter in Aquarius.

The Comanchero gang member in Chart 12 has a grand trine with Uranus, Neptune, and Mercury. It is actually a kite formation, with Pluto opposite the Mercury, conjunct the Midheaven, and sextiling Uranus and Neptune. The Devil's Disciple member in Chart 13, once the president of his club, has a Moon/Uranus conjunction opposite Jupiter in Sagittarius, Sagittarius rising, and Sun and Mercury in Aquarius. The second Devil's Disciple, Chart 14, also has a Sun, Mercury, and Venus conjunction, this time in Aquarius, opposite Pluto and Saturn. The fire element shows up in his Sagittarius ascendant and Aries Moon. Interested students can peruse these charts in more depth, and, if they are especially brave or foolhardy, increase the sample somewhat.

Although only a solar chart would be possible, one last example may be of interest to the student. It was that of a biker, Devil's Disciple president Danny Coates, who epitomized the biker's code of "live fast, die young." He was born 6/21/44 in Boston, Mass. He died of a combination of gunshot wound and auto crash in Fresno, CA at 5:08 AM on 8/6/85. I asked psychically the purpose of that death, and was told it was to learn as quickly and dramatically as possible the lesson of self-will run riot. Also, it was for his group to learn it as well—so Uranian!

Now that I've courageously pigeon-holed the bikers as perpetually adolescent and in cowardice declined to nominate any other group, let me say that there is quite possibly nothing wrong with being a perpetual adolescent. On the personal level, it looks counterproductive, but on the societal level, it may keep us all honest, pointing out the truth about the emperor's new clothes. Uranians are the joker in the deck, the fool in the tarot.

Furthermore, there's a frozen slice of perpetual adolescent in all of us, waiting to defrost. Uranus transits in general provide the electricity to

Chart 9

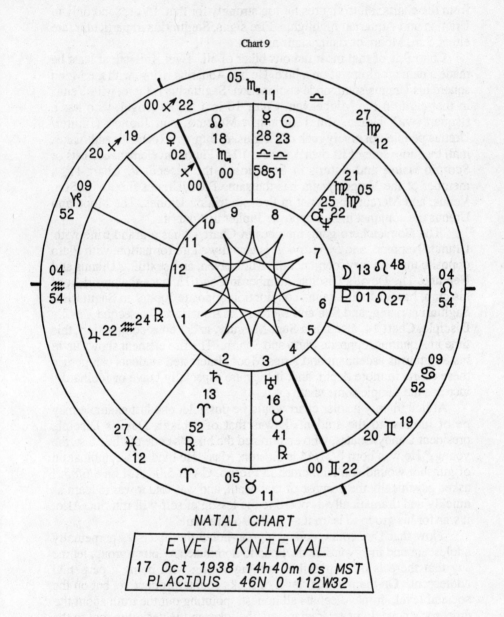

NATAL CHART

EVEL KNIEVAL
17 Oct 1938 14h40m 0s MST
PLACIDUS 46N 0 112W32

Chart 10

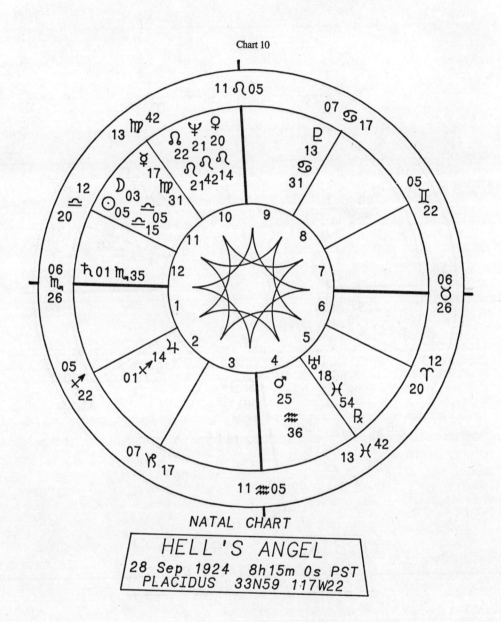

NATAL CHART

HELL'S ANGEL
28 Sep 1924   8h15m 0s PST
PLACIDUS   33N59 117W22

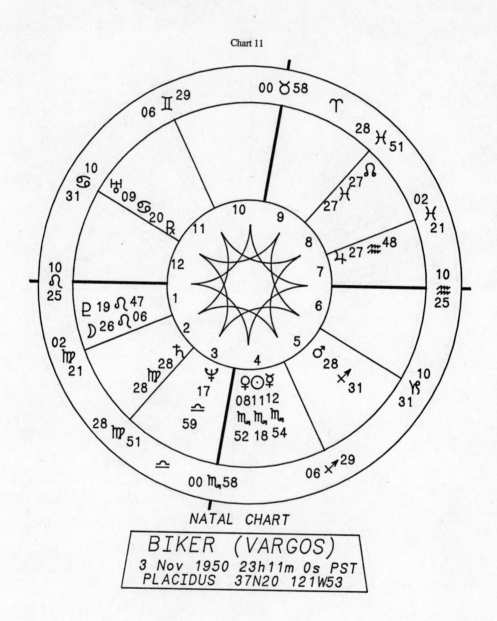

Chart 11

NATAL CHART

BIKER (VARGOS)
3 Nov 1950 23h11m 0s PST
PLACIDUS 37N20 121W53

Chart 12

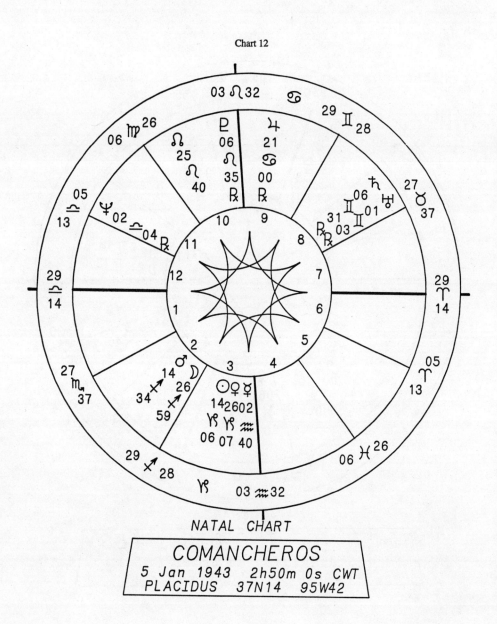

NATAL CHART

COMANCHEROS
5 Jan 1943   2h50m 0s CWT
PLACIDUS   37N14   95W42

Chart 13

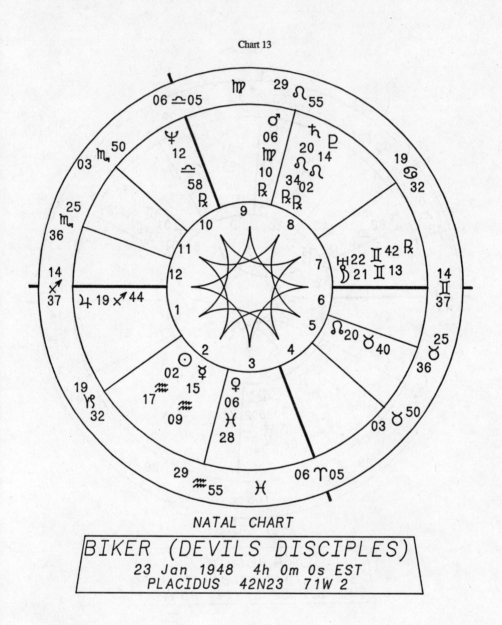

NATAL CHART

BIKER (DEVILS DISCIPLES)
23 Jan 1948   4h 0m 0s EST
PLACIDUS   42N23   71W 2

Chart 14

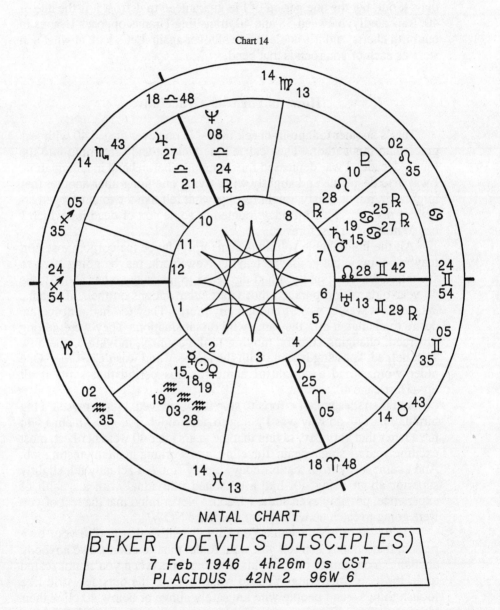

NATAL CHART

BIKER (DEVILS DISCIPLES)
7 Feb 1946   4h26m 0s CST
PLACIDUS   42N 2   96W 6

thaw it out, but the one period of life guaranteed to defrost it is the age of 40. Repeatedly, between 38 and 40, transiting Uranus opposes Uranus in our birth charts, and it's adolescence all over again. Let's look at what's in store as each of you rounds that bend.

How to Turn 40 Gracefully

That's another tongue-in-cheek title. No one ever turned 40 with less grace than this author. They carried me kicking and screaming into the fourth decade. I was depressed for six months beforehand in anticipation. I was also desperate and slightly wild, trying one thing after another that might suit, might satisfy, might resolve what felt like the total untogetherness of my life. That birthday loomed as some sort of deadline which I had to meet or be lost forever.

All the unthinkable solutions came up. Maybe the corporate sector, maybe having a baby, maybe leaving New York, maybe going back to school, maybe… Finally, I had the sense to interview other about-to-be 40-year-olds who'd pursued those particular options on their life paths. Whatever it was, it wasn't enough any more. They too had a desperate desire to change it all, the same wild dissatisfaction. They were getting divorced, changing careers, moving to the country, moving to the city. That helped, knowing it came with the territory and wasn't just me. One older woman had a delightful name for this period that sums it all up—Hurricane 40.

And then, despite all efforts to stop it, 40 arrived. I gave myself a big birthday party—no way was I going to go through it alone. An aunt sent me a letter that very day, saying that the years after 40 were her best, most exciting years—single again, traveling, and working in an interesting job. And I came away from that birthday slightly smug. I actually felt slightly superior about being 40, like a seasoned individual with a wealth of experience, possibly even some wisdom. Never mind that the rest of you were going to catch up with me—I was there NOW!

Being 40 grows on you. You start to realize that you're your own person, that nobody can tell you what to do, that you don't owe anybody anything. You start to explore this freedom, and, when you're not scared to death, it's exhilarating. You do what looks to the outside world like foolish things—and people who are safely above or below 40 click their tongues and say, "You're acting like a teenager." And you ARE, but now you're a teenager with a car, money of your own, and a bit of experience to keep from making the ghastliest mistakes. No doubt, all your life you've done what "they" said. Now you decide to invent your own rules, find a new life, get a fresh start.

Pop psychologists will be muttering, "Mid-life crisis." Astrologers will be saying, "That's Uranus...and that's Uranus...and that's Uranus too." Of course, both are absolutely right. The mid-life crisis—at least this particular part of it—IS Uranus. The painful itch of dissatisfaction, the wild experimentation, the exhilarating freedom, the being, at long last, your own person.

Although Uranus transits, at whatever age, provoke identity crises, the Uranus opposition to natal Uranus between 38 and 40 is special—an identity crisis shared by all in your age group. (Fitting, isn't it, for Uranus, the planet of groups?) And you'd better stick close to your group during it, because no one else understands. To people under 37, the age of 40 is as unreal as death, something that only happens to other unfortunates. The 38-year-olds, unless they're extremely precocious, are busy denying it will ever happen to them. The 42-year-olds are already immersed in what comes next. (I won't tell you what that is—it would be giving away the plot.)

In my particular age group, the crisis was attenuated by belonging to that rather frustrated generation born with the Uranus/Saturn conjunction of 1941-42. A tad young for the conservative Fifties, a tad old for the radical Sixties. Maybe in it, but never truly part of it, and working all the harder to belong. (Here the pronoun IT is intentionally vague and refers to either the Fifties or the Sixties, whichever generation you primarily identified with.) Betwixt and between, and, yes, WE SET IT UP THAT WAY so we could bridge the generation gap, smooth the edges, be a unifying force. We were needed but it was often painful. Now that we're all over 40 and past the Uranus opposition to that conjunction, we are free at last, "free at last, thank God Almighty, we're free at last!"

What has become clear, as I watch people coming through that pass called 40, is that this particular identity crisis is the quintessence of identity crises, something we can all learn from. For most of us, what passes for an identity is not the true self (the Sun) or what is unique to us (Uranus), but our roles. Roles—formally contracted duties and responsibilities—are Saturnian in nature. In Saturn fashion, they give us structure, but as time goes on they crystallize us, rigidify our behavior, limit our definitions of ourselves, and proscribe our options. We define ourselves as much by our limitations (Saturn) as by our capabilities. Uranus follows Saturn in the solar system, and Uranus transits are antidotes for Saturnian rigidification. They often bring crucial ruptures in our roles which lead to identity crises.

At 40, the rupture is often that our children don't need us any more. Often they're Uranian creatures too—adolescents or young adults—and are struggling for freedom from us. Our own parents, if they are around 61, are having Uranus square to natal Uranus, an upheaval that changes our relationship to them. Sometimes the rupture in roles is that we've outgrown our mates or our mates have outgrown us; we've outgrown the job or it's outgrown us technologically (Uranus again). We no longer need or want the rings of Saturn around us, and we itch to discover all over again who we really are, separate from our roles. (If we are unwilling, through fear or inertia, to venture forth, the universe boots us out of the nest all the same, by creating forceful ruptures.)

Another way identity is limited by Saturn is through our concepts about age. Our culture is so focused on preserving and glorifying youth, that becoming 40 is needlessly difficult. It is the undisputed marker of middle age, when you can no longer deny it. We no longer value older people for their contribution or for wisdom gained from experience. We think over 40 is over the hill, so the 40-year-old naturally thinks it is all downhill from here. To be 40 is to be a failure in a contest which only youth and beauty can win. Having money helps, since that's another winning entry, but even the well-to-do have real discomfort about becoming 40. How very sad that is. It is only in the time since 40 that I have come to cherish my uniqueness and the special things about me that years of experience have brought into being.

Age has its role definitions too. The 14-year-old is supposed to have dates and go to football games, the 22-year-old, fresh out of college, is supposed to venture out into the world, while the 30-year-old is already supposed to be successful. The 40-year-old disturbs others because the behavior is not age-appropriate. We were supposed to have done all that when we were adolescents, but our parents or peer group wouldn't let us, so we're doing it now. We're rocking the boat, in that reprehensible Uranian way. Perhaps it will pacify the rest of you to know that around 43, when Saturn opposes natal Saturn, we will settle down again.

Uranus is actually only part of the picture. The rest of what happens to you between 38 and 42 has been done to such perfection by Doris Hebel that one hesitates to do it at all. Hers is the finest exposition of life cycles available today, and you can read it in her book, *Celestial Psychology: An Astrological Guide to Growth and Transformation* If Doris comes to your town and you don't go hear her, you're a fool. Along with several others, Doris points out that the period between 38 and 42 is unique, in that several astrological cycles peak at that point.

Uranus forms an opposition to natal Uranus between 38 and 40, creating the syndrome described above. Beginning slightly later, Neptune squares natal Neptune, signifying profound disillusionment with whatever you've been illusioned by. Somewhere in there, depending on the individual, the progressed Moon is opposite natal Moon, coinciding with lunar changes like the children leaving home, the necessity to become a parent to your own parents, or menopause. From 40 to 42, Pluto squares natal Pluto, colloquially termed "shit or get off the pot." At around 43 or 44,

Saturn is opposite natal Saturn, making you feel your years and an urgency to accomplish your life purpose. (We've been drawing parallels between this period and adolescence. At around age 14, Saturn is also opposite natal Saturn and progressed Moon opposite natal Moon.)

No other phase of life has so many cycles coming together, so it is crucial and unique. Doris Hebel feels this age is when you make the decision to embrace life and live it fully or else slowly begin to die. Justice cannot be done to her three-hour workshop in a paragraph, but this brief summary shows how complex this age is, a turning point where one set of roles and expectations is finishing and a whole new life can begin.

Living Through 14 and 40

Neither 14 or 40 are pathological conditions. They are what sociologists call NORMATIVE crises, that is, everyone who lives long enough experiences them. And, everyone who lives long enough also lives through them. Like all Uranian earthquakes, these two eventually subside. The remedy MALLOW is for both puberty and menopause, for the mid-life crisis, for making friends, and for the fear of aging. SAGEBRUSH is for shedding outmoded self-concepts and establishing a true identity, while offsetting false identifications and influences. Homeopathically, the best remedy for Uranian periods is to be Uranian. Allow yourself freedom to explore new ways of being, learn from others in your peer group who are going through the same thing, and let go of old self-concepts which may be keeping you from discovering who you are becoming. Like all Uranian periods, it can be exciting, so enjoy yourself—all too soon, it will pass.

1 The material in this section was originally printed as "Getting Through the Trying Teens, *Astrology Guide* (March, 1980), p. 80.
2 Michel and Francoise Gauquelin, *The Gauquelin Book of American Charts,* (San Diego, CA: ACS),1982.

CHAPTER EIGHT

URANUS TRANSITS: SURVIVING DIVORCE AND OTHER EARTHQUAKES

Uranus transits signify abrupt, often radical changes—common events are divorce, quitting a job or getting fired, accidents, and explosions of suppressed anger. Not everyone will undergo such drastic events, yet the status quo is always threatened, and as a result these are unsettled yet exciting times. We will see that astrology can help us understand their purpose, and by anticipatory work, prevent truly traumatic shakeups. We will explore the causes of common Uranian events.

Such times ARE stressful. Researchers have found that the unexpected event is the most difficult to cope with. We are less prepared, more stunned, and more grief stricken by that bolt out of the blue than by expected changes such as children leaving home, retirement, and the death of a parent. All changes are stressful, but unexpected events are shocking, forcing change on us instantly. They jolt us like earthquakes.

Earthquakes as a Metaphor for Uranus Transits

I have long considered earthquakes a good metaphor for Uranus transits, but after living in California a couple of years, it got harder to be detached about that particular image. The biggest earthquake we had in that time was a 20-second roller in which each second was separate and distinct. Part of me was excited...IT was FINALLY happening...and part of me wanted to cry because I was so afraid. Many Uranus transits carry that same mixture of excitement and terror. We may not know the difference between excitement and fear, as they feel so similar. I can recall saying I was nervous about making my first trip to my home town in 20 years, and my friend saying, "You're not nervous, you're excited," and he was right.

Earthquakes SEEM to come out of the blue, and so do things that happen under Uranus, but that's not the truth. Earthquakes happen when sufficient pressure builds up along a fault, as a way of releasing the tension. Two planes are jammed together without enough slippage to move freely. Significantly, they are shaped rather like the glyph for Aquarius, which Uranus rules: The same thing often happens along fault lines of our lives. Where Uranus is, there is the possibility of a split or underground schism when we don't give ourselves enough freedom, when we're too confined. The outside world sees us going along day by day, yet inside the need for change keeps building, until it's unbearable and an explosion occurs. Afterwards, despite being shaken up, there is a sense of relief, a release of tension.

For instance, with violence, there is often a long, slow buildup before the event. Violence is an extreme reaction to extreme pressure, but every Uranian event—divorce, getting fired, moving—arises from coercion to maintain the status quo, which ultimately results in a personal earthquake. Just as earthquakes really don't occur out of the blue, neither do relationship breakups or blowups on the job...they build and build. Uranus takes 84 years to orbit the Sun, so in the course of a lifetime you'll have quakes or tremors in every area. Where is your fault line right now?

These ideas may sound scary, but only from the perspective that says change is a catastrophe. Earthquakes, volcanic eruptions, and other forceful happenings in nature serve the purpose of providing an escape valve, and so do Uranian events.

It's only when we persist in building along fault lines in the earth that earthquakes destroy so much; it's only when we persist in building along our own personal fault lines that truly destructive things happen. Astrology can identify those fault lines and the times when too much pressure has built up. Forewarned, we can do something constructive, can work with the forward movement, rather than resist change until it is forced upon us.

Much energy is freed by the personal earthquake. It releases tension, leaving us energized because we're not putting all our energy into resistance. There's often a sense of relief, such as when a couple who have been headed for a battle or a breakup for a long time get a divorce, or when we've hated our job for a long time and finally quit. It's a relief to have it done with, to move forward again. "I've been dreading it for so long, I'm glad it's over." There are a series of aftershocks, as various parts of our lives realign to compensate. For instance, a change in work can bring about a new identity or independence to which friends, family, and lovers have to adjust.

The Function of Uranus Transits

The behavior of people under Uranus transits LOOKS crazy, wild, unpredictable, and unconventional. But as strange as they look, there is method to the madness. The purpose is to develop Uranian parts of their being, like the capacity to stand as separate individuals rather than following the crowd like automatons. They develop their own separate identity, expressing that which is unique about themselves. Uranus is about consciousness, and the upsetting things that happen under Uranus transits are the CONSEQUENCES of our desire to remain UNCONSCIOUS, especially unconscious of changes that we need to make.

For example, people having Uranus transits to the Midheaven, sixth, or tenth house may wind up getting fired, then go through a period of instability in employment, say six months with one job, three in another totally unrelated field, and a year somewhere entirely different. As unstable as this may look on the outside, such people are conducting a series of experiments to find out exactly who they are and what they're capable of. Uranus transits are a time when they try out all the WHAT IFS and the IF ONLIES.

Uranus and Individuation

I've discussed individuation in earlier books, so we won't consider it at length, but nonetheless, it has great relevance here. Throughout life, under Uranus transits, we go through many births where we leave safety and security behind to try something new. These are times when we become more separate. When we go to school, to advance our consciousness, we leave the womb of our family behind a few hours a day. When we go out on our own, we leave that womb behind for good. Uranus rules both separations and independence, and we experience insecurity at each of these separations, yet once we master the new demands, we function more independently than ever.

INDIVIDUATION is Eric Fromm's term for this process of becoming more and more separate. Leaving behind safe, familiar territory is frightening, so most of us have to be pushed. Uranus transits are the push we need. They shock us out of our rut and make us suddenly want a different life, scorning the old. We go overboard at first in trying to establish new patterns, but ultimately settle into a milder, more comfortable sense of liberated selfhood. The thing that once nurtured us, we wind up throwing away—the umbilical chord is useless ten minutes after birth.

Because social pressure to conform is so stifling and constricting, we suppress our true selves at a heavy cost. The more startling and SEEMINGLY uncharacteristic the behavior during a Uranus transit, the more constricted and suppressed the true self has been (Scorpio on the tenth house of the Aquarian wheel). Impulsive, rebellious behaviors do not represent the true self, however, just the lengths people feel they have to go in order to establish the right to be themselves.

Divorce and Separation

DIVORCE is one of those words of power which once spoken cannot be unspoken. When one of the marriage partners says they want a divorce, there's a kind of divorce, even if the couple stays together. It's as bad as saying, "I NEVER LOVED YOU." Thus, I don't predict divorce—I may predict a crisis in the relationship calling for readjustment, but I don't plant that seed. Instead I discuss the underlying difficulty, which is that both partners need to grow and develop interests of their own. There's a need for greater independence. I ask questions to assess how much dependency is present in the relationship. Where it is stifling, I talk about the need for greater self-reliance and discuss ways for that to happen. If there is great resistance to growth, I suggest that the partner could be growing tired of the dependency and this could cause problems in the relationship. I may suggest individual or couple therapy.

These are my observations of what seems to happen when couples split. The presence of the Uranus transit suggests that one or both has grown in consciousness and is ready to leave the formerly comfortable dependency behind. Perhaps the wife has begun taking classes or working and is beginning to get a new sense of self. Finding oneself more capable changes the balance of the relationship, so that it must adjust or ultimately end. At other times, the partner begins to resent being mommy or daddy, and insists the other assume a more adult role. The other may be extremely threatened, clinging or restricting the person's freedom, so pressure builds up to a split. The partner who feels constricted may use that Uranian phrase, "I need my space."

During a Uranus transit to Venus or the seventh house, an exciting romantic figure may come on the scene. THE OTHER WOMAN or the other man, THE HOME WRECKER. It's THEM that caused all the trouble, right? It's all their fault the marriage broke up. They connived and sneaked around and stole your man or woman, right? WRONG! The other woman or man is a patsy who is USED by a partner to do what the partner doesn't have the courage to do—to end the marriage.

Maybe there hasn't been anything in particular to complain about, but people feel stagnant or that their individuality is stifled in the relationship. Most people won't get divorced over that, won't rock the boat and risk anything new, but there's dissatisfaction and restlessness. Along comes someone exciting, someone who validates their identity, recognizes how special they are, and helps them experiment with new ways of being. As with any other Uranian experiment, they often wind up discarding it after a new identity and new behaviors are comfortably established. The other woman, or the other man, is very often tossed aside once he or she has served a purpose.

I call such people TRANSITIONAL OBJECTS. Like teddy bears, they are there to make us comfortable as we grow a little away from mommy or daddy, but we put them aside when we feel safer. Uranian relationships outside marriage are often for similar purposes, like helping us move across country or study something new. The charge, the excitement—Leo on the seventh—is what they teach about ourselves and our potentials.

Is Uranus inevitable? Are relationship breakups seen in the chart preventable? Yes, if both partners are willing to be more Uranian, to pursue their individuality, independence, and uniqueness during the transit. Conceivably, they could actually become more exciting to one another and get closer. But that takes work and courage.

The aftermath (aftershocks) of divorce or separation are also interestingly Uranian. How wild and unstable that first year is, like the reactions of the Aquarius Rising wheel. Yet, for the woman who went from her parents' home to her husband's, who never experienced being on her own, the result is more individuation. The process is stressful, beyond a doubt, yet the end result is an increase in consciousness and more of a separate identity.

Le Plus Ce Change....

The French have a saying, "Le plus ce change, le plus c'est le meme chose," which means, "The more something changes, the more it remains the same." This is frequently true of the seemingly drastic changes people go through under Uranus transits. This is a series of changes, in fact, as the same transit happens three times by retrograde and direct motion. We do something that to outward appearances looks radically different. We quit our insurance job and go to work in a disco, we bleach our hair, we move to California, we stop going out with bankers and start going out with bikers...or vice versa. I'VE CHANGED, I'M COMPLETELY DIFFERENT, CAN'T YOU SEE?

And, yet, le plus ce change. Somehow the biker constricts our freedom the same way the banker did. The boss is just as tough on us in the disco as the son of a gun at the insurance office was. We don't feel any more attractive just because we're blonder or thinner or reek of Chanel. And we have just as many lonely Saturday nights in California as we did back home. Everything has changed and nothing is any different. So the next time Uranus hits the same place, we try something ENTIRELY different, and it winds up being entirely the same.

In the Twelve Step programs like Alcoholics Anonymous and Narcotics Anonymous, the members call changes like these Geographics.

People with a drinking problem believe they'd stop if they moved somewhere else, or had a different job or a different wife. So they get the different wife or job, and the drinking goes on just the same as always. Obviously, the problem is that they take themselves along when they move or change jobs or leave their mates. They've projected responsibility for their limitations onto others, rather than accepting them as their own. (All of this, once more, is like Capricorn on the twelfth house of the Aquarius Rising wheel.)

If so few changes are real, why do we make them? What impels us to pack up and move cross country or to leave behind the job that gave us security for 20 years? What a lot of energy—and what a lot of courage—major moves like these take! Uranus transits are a time of experimentation—not foolishness, not flightiness, but the Higher Self at work. We need precisely to understand that it is not THEM but US, that holds us back. We need to see that WE are the cause of our difficulties, not our circumstances.

"You Cannot Get There From Here."

Another phenomenon I've observed with Uranus transits is what I call "You cannot get there from here." On the first hit, people leave their little home towns, their families, and everybody they've known since grade school and move all the way to California. They burn their bridges, have their going away party, and say goodbye forever. On the second hit, they decide they don't like California after all, so they move to Florida. On the third hit, they move again, this time 20 miles (or 20 blocks) away from where they started. Moving is just an example—I've observed precisely the same process with other areas of life, like jobs and love affairs.

This series of events is really puzzling to people who are watching it, and equally puzzling to the person doing the moving around. They think, and you agree, that you're really crazy, mixed up, and floundering. Yet, there is purpose behind it. The purpose is that YOU CANNOT GET THERE FROM HERE. What I mean is, you were so fixed in the old environment, conforming to others' expectations, that it was difficult to change and express the self you were becoming. The form of the past was too confining. In order to be even a little bit different, you had to move far from home, to a place where no one had any expectations of you at all, so you felt free to cut loose and experiment.

Despite what I've already said about geographic cures, moving can help you be free of old definitions of yourselves, so you can change in directions you've already identified, except that the old structures and expectations made it difficult. In a new place (or a new job or a new relationship), you can experiment with new identities, many of which will be discarded along the way. Capricorn on the twelfth shows the need to renounce structure in order to find it.

When you've had a chance to be your own person, when the new behaviors feel comfortable, then it's safe to move back nearer to where you started. You couldn't have made the small move without the bigger, more extreme one. Force and distance were required, a Declaration of Independence was needed. You had to make a statement about being a separate individual. The whole process is like Jung's concept of the pendulum, which says that the further you are on one side, the further in the opposite direction you need to go in order to wind up balanced in the middle. A Uranus transit is often the pendulum swinging, wildly at first.

So What's It All For?

Even when change isn't so drastic in the end, it puts you in touch with who you are. When all the outside limitations are gone, all the people and situations around you that you think are holding you back, then what you are left with is YOU. And you get to see that you are the builder and designer of the structure you find yourself in. Even if the earthquake has leveled it, you may once more build the old structure or one remarkably like it unless you consciously redesign it. Part of how you come to see this is that you may reconstruct the structure two or three times during the series of Uranus transits, yet you build it so flimsily in your rush to get somewhere new that the merest tremor knocks it over. You've used cardboard, and part of you knows very well it's cardboard, but you do it anyway because that's how you learn.

Specific Uranus Transits

Usually during a Uranus transit, many things happen at once—some wonderful, some awful, some bizarre. You hit the lottery, you break an arm, you run into the old, lost love of your life, and your best friend reveals she's gay. It's like opening a popcorn popper that's going full tilt. Things fly all over the place. They say to expect the unexpected, and that Uranus transits are unpredictable, so I'm not going to predict them here.

What also seem to come up with Uranus transits, are issues. With Neptune and Pluto, you get FEELINGS, with Uranus it's ISSUES. Of course, there are feelings behind the issues, but we try to be detached. It's the principle of the thing. We've already been talking about the kinds of issues you may be dealing with, so the chapter as a whole can be useful for those undergoing major aspects.

With Uranus to the Sun, the issue is finding a new self-definition, as opposed to that which parents, friends, and society have imposed on you. Whatever they expect of you, you will do the opposite for a while, until you "find yourself." With Uranus to the Moon, the break with past, family, and roots may be even more profound, sometimes involving a major residential change. Emotions may also be tumultuous, and there is considerable experimenting with feelings that have never been seen as comfortable or safe before. With Uranus to Mercury, new and radically different ideas come into your life, often with a crowd of new people to learn them from.

With Uranus to Venus, the issue is "space," as in "I need my..." Who needs the space? Maybe you, maybe your partner, maybe that exciting new love interest. Give it or lose. When Mars is involved, the popcorn flying all over the place may be anger, so it's time to learn a new way of handling it, not suppressing it and not acting on it rashly. Assertiveness is a key. With Uranus to Jupiter, you'll be more Uranian than the Uranians and more sure you're right than the Jupiterians, but there'll be lots of excitement, possibly mainly intellectual or philosophical. Uranus to Saturn wants to break down old structures which have grown too rigidified.

Uranus transits to its own natal position bring all the Uranus issues discussed in these several chapters to the forefront. Uranus to Neptune is a natural high, high on spirit—unless, of course, you are excessively prone to other kinds of highs, in which case there could be an explosion because of your habits. Uranus aspects to Pluto bring the necessity to let go of the past and of controlling behavior as well as defiance, otherwise power plays could become very troublesome. Uranus to the MC/IC can bring a restless desire to change jobs, residence, and the relationship to the past. Uranus to the ASC/DSC means a new way of presenting yourself in the world and in your most intimate relationships, letting go of an old image and giving yourself and others a great deal more freedom.

Flower Essences for Uranus

There are several remedies which are helpful with the kinds of identity crises Uranus transits often bring. MULLEIN is for being true to oneself and fulfilling one's true potential. SAGEBRUSH offsets false identification and influences; for example, an identification with parents that causes a false or outdated self-concept. SAGUARO gives clarity in relationship to paternal and authority figures. QUAKING GRASS, on the other hand, blends individual egos to produce group harmony.

CHERRY PLUM helps with explosive Uranian states where there is fear of uncontrolled temper or of losing control and doing something harmful to yourself or others. RESCUE REMEDY, a combination of several Bach products, is available in most health food stores, and is excellent to keep in your first aid kit for a crisis, physical or emotional. STAR OF BETHLEHEM heals shocks and traumas, no matter how long ago. WALNUT is invaluable for people in transition, such as those under Uranus transits. WILD OAT helps with that feeling of restlessness and dissatisfaction with not having found one's niche in life.

For those who live too much in their heads, whether under a natal aspect or a transiting one, there are many remedies. MANZANITA helps with groundedness and being at home in the body, NASTURTIUM lends earthly expressiveness, for those who are overly intellectual and lack vitality. NECTARINE increases New Age consciousness, yet provides balance. LEMON brings clarity of thought, a sense of relaxation, and a release of stress.

For the Uranian type by birth, there are several remedies which can lessen the harder forms of the syndrome. ROCK WATER is for those who martyr themselves in pursuit of an ideal and are rigid and inflexible. VERVAIN helps those who become incensed at injustices and who are fanatical, high-strung, straining people. WATER VIOLET is for the aloof sort who do not meddle in the affairs of others but are very capable and involved in their own work. SHOOTING STAR is for overcoming alienation among those who feel they don't fit in, so that they feel at home on earth and with others. SWEET PEA eases social conflict, such as the antisocial personality or acting out teenager.

CHAPTER NINE

URANUS AND ACCIDENTS:
THEIR PURPOSE AND PREVENTION

Aspects by transiting Uranus are often read as possible accidents, for instance Uranus to the Ascendant, to a planet in the first, sixth or twelfth house, or to Mars. Because of an accident-prone aspect in my chart—a conjunction of Venus, Uranus, and Saturn—I've had many minor accidents in the form of falls caused by twisted ankles. Due to the presence of Venus in the combination (or maybe just to sheer practice), I fall well and am never seriously hurt. Observing my state of mind just prior to an occurrence led to some interesting discoveries. For instance, they tend to happen immediately after a rebellious thought. Becoming interested in the phenomenon, I studied accidents and found them very complex. My findings are presented so astrologers can discuss accident-prone aspects with clients and conceivably prevent serious injuries.

Why Accidents Happen: Give Me a Break!

As we will see, few accidents are purely accidental. Instead they serve important purposes related to Uranus, such as freedom, rebellion, breaking away from the past, and developing individuality. The psychologically inclined believe accidents arise from self-destructive urges. I find that although they cause pain and disruption, in the long run, they are not DEstructive but CONstructive, not the UNconscious at work but the SUPERconscious.

Questioning people who had serious injuries, I find they often happen when people aren't true to themselves. They're stuck in a situation they find oppressive or alien. Unable to break away, they're restless, frustrated, and rebellious. In addition to broken body parts, the accident creates a break from the situation. There's method to the madness—it serves the Uranian purpose of getting free. An accident, even a minor one, should be a warning that you're stifling your individuality.

A case in point would be Princess Grace's stroke and fatal accident. There were many reports in the year or two before that she was having serious marital problems and great unhappiness over her children. Yet, no one resigns from the job of Princess of Monaco—it's just not done—so she may have felt stuck in an untenable position from which she could not escape. My feeling is that the accident/stroke was her way of getting a divorce. (Divorce, of course, is also related to Uranus.) The medical term for a stroke is cerebral vascular accident, and strokes are also indicated astrologically by Uranus. Metaphysically, circulatory problems are related to a lack of freedom. A stroke is often a strike, a way of protesting your working conditions in life.

As many have remarked, Grace's chart shows no clear indication of her accident or death, except that Jupiter, natally in her eighth house, had recently crossed her ascendant. Many astrologers have noted supposedly benign Jupiter prominent at the time of death. Either we don't understand Jupiter as well as we think, or we don't understand death. According to her birth certificate, as noted in Lois Rodden's, *Profiles of Women,* she was born 11/12/29 at 5:31 AM in Philadelphia, 75W10; 39N57. She died on 9/16/82.

To give another illustration, Debra Winger had always wanted to act, yet was studying for a more practical career in sociology. A near-fatal car wreck when she was 18 left her blind and partially paralyzed, requiring numerous hospitalizations over the course of a year. After Debra recovered, she decided to try for stardom. She dropped out of college and enrolled in acting classes. Within three years she was getting parts in commercials, followed by such major movie roles as Urban Cowboy and Terms of Endearment. About her near-fatal mishap, Debra says, "I look at my accident as a huge chunk of grace. It propelled me into doing what I wanted to do." She was born 5/16/55 in Columbus, Ohio, but I don't have the time. There is a tight t-square with Venus at 25 Aries, Jupiter and Uranus at 24 and 25 of Cancer, and Neptune at 26 Libra. I would speculate that Jupiter and Uranus are in the tenth, near the MC (fitting for television's former Wonder Woman), and Neptune is in the first, near the Ascendant. The transits for the date of her accident, on 12/31/73, show Uranus at 27 Libra, just finishing the t-square.

Uranus has to do with major changes, so the break that the accident creates—the time of recuperation—often initiates an abrupt halt and a new beginning. Two of my friends who are chiropractors decided on this career after serious collisions hospitalized them for considerable periods of time. (No doubt, there was also an element of rebellion against traditional medicine involved in this choice!) The chart of one of them will be presented later with the case examples.

The recovery period is an interval of discovery, in which individuals have free time to find out their own particular uniqueness and genius. There are many cases where the recuperation period helped individuals find their true paths. Herbalist Jeanne Rose, who wrote a number of books on the subject, began studying herbs while confined to bed after an accident. Rosemary Brown is an English medium who channels new masterpieces by Bach and other classical composers and most recently of John Lennon. She had been told of her gift of mediumship but only began developing it seriously while recovering from an accident. These events often serve the Uranian purpose of turning us away from what is NOT US and helping us discover and express our own personal genius.

The Aquarius Rising Wheel and Accidents

Further insights come from studying the Aquarius Rising wheel. With Aquarius on the first house, there is an element of defiance—victims are usually breaking safety rules and believe rules don't apply to them. Wrecks often happen when people are in a reckless state of mind, craving excitement. Like violence or other Uranian events, they are explosions relieving built-up tension. Times of turmoil and excitement are more likely to produce them.

Pisces on the second house shows that the payoff is often a spiritual one, a twelfth house retreat which leads to cultivation of creativity and relatedness to the Higher Self. The people whose stories are given above used their recuperation this way. Aries on the third suggests that accidents can be a way of communicating anger. People under accident-prone transits could prevent injury by learning to express anger more directly. Taurus on the fourth shows that there is something of value to be gained in the end (if only through the inevitable big-bucks lawsuit) and also that accidents are like grounding an electric shock, bringing people down to earth.

You can learn a great deal from going completely around the wheel, but three houses are particularly interesting. Cancer on the sixth correlates with research findings reported in psychiatrist Dr. Arnold Leiber's book, *The Lunar Effect,* that women are much more accident prone when premenstrual. J.E. Davidson of the Sandia Laboratories found that accident rates correlated with phases of the Moon. Another especially telling placement is Scorpio on the tenth house, which shows the purpose or goal. Many fatal accidents are only thinly disguised suicides. In fact, many are actual suicides, written off as mishaps. In particular, psychiatrists find that teenagers' accidents, especially repeated ones, are suicide attempts, as they have no other way of breaking out of an intolerable situation. Suicide is due to murderous rage which people cannot express and instead turn against the self. These circumstances often arise when people feel totally controlled by authority figures or life. Davidson's results showed a tendency for more accident-proneness at the same phase of the Moon you were born under and the opposite one. For example, at both the full and new Moon if you were born under either of them, or at the first or third quarter if you were born under either.

Another Scorpionic intent, whether personal or cosmic, could be liberation from the body without having to suffer from an illness. This may be true even of mass disasters, such as airplane crashes, in that the Higher Self of the individual could know what is coming and choose to take this opportunity to be free. Where the accident is not fatal, it is often TRANS-FORMATIVE, putting us in touch with mortality and making us focus more intensely on goals.

A final set of insights from the wheel corresponds with Capricorn on the twelfth. We often have accidents when we are testing our limits, wanting to go beyond ourselves, yet ignoring limits and reality—not using fear constructively. The hidden purpose is to ground people, block them from doing something that is not good for them, and make them more aware of their true life goals. Serious injuries also give people an unarguable "I cannot" limitation when they don't want to do something, particularly in the way of a career. Men who have back injuries, for example, say "I cannot do further manual labor" and they get retrained for something they like better. Macho expectations of physical prowess make it hard to say this directly, so it's face-saving to have a physical reason. Since this is the twelfth house, the purpose is unconscious.

When Are Accidents Likely to Happen?

In chewing over the whys and wherefores, I read what people in the accident business have found out. A study by Penn State University Institute of Public Safety shows that people under a great deal of stress are likely candidates. They also found something I've long suspected—that a series of minor mishaps can be a danger signal that a major accident is on the way. I came to this conclusion after discussing accident-prone transits with a great many clients who said they'd already had a series of near-misses, as the Uranus aspect made its three or more passes or drew near to exact. I tell clients to pay particular attention to near-misses and use them as signals that in order to prevent serious injury, they must work on Uranian issues (which we discuss in detail during the consultation).

Dr. Stanley Aronson of Brown University studied 766 traffic deaths and found that divorced, separated, or single people were far more likely to have fatal accidents. Haven't you had clients who said they lost their job, their wife left them, and they wrecked their car, all on the same day? Uranus transits, of course, can correlate with divorce or separation, so when a client is undergoing a separation, it might be well to discuss accident possibilities as well.

Uranus aspects to Ascendant/Descendant or MC/IC axis may be most likely to result in such a combination of events.

Adolescence, a Uranian time of life, with its turbulent struggle for identity, increases the likelihood of accidents. More than half of all teenage deaths—two thirds for boys—are from accidents. Dr. Dunbar Flanders feels that youngsters who have trouble making themselves understood are practically forced to do something, smash something, or hurt themselves to get attention.[1]

A Japanese meridian therapy practitioner told me he feels accidents often occur when there is an energy block in the body. You hit or drop something on the area, even repeatedly, to stimulate that meridian. The blow releases the blockage. An astrological contribution to this theory is that Uranus is connected with electricity and the flow of energy. Accident-prone people are strongly Uranian, and sometimes, with Uranians, there is something a little wrong with the wiring.

Explosions of violence are also Uranian events, and it strikes me that perhaps the places we get punched or hurt in fights are body parts that physically—or metaphysically—need stimulating. A blow to the solar plexus, it would seem, is a reminder not to let ego get out of hand. (IT STRIKES ME is also a Uranian metaphor for those sudden hits of consciousness that happen when our minds work in Uranian ways.)

It is also interesting to note when accidents DO NOT occur. In 1976, when a Uranus/Saturn square from Leo to Scorpio was in orb most of the year, newspapers reported that accidents dropped to the lowest level in 14 years, or half a Saturn cycle. Apparently Saturn's natural caution and reality testing helps ground people and prevent accidents. Perhaps it also gives people the self-discipline to work seriously on their goals.

Chart Examples to Study

Singer Julio Iglesias had his life turned around by a serious accident at the age of 19 which threatened to paralyze him for life. He was a star soccer player studying for a career in law when it occurred in Madrid in July, 1963. He was paralyzed from the waist down but stubbornly—defiantly—refused to use a wheelchair or to give up. Mobilization of this kind of defiance, a positive expression of Uranus's rebelliousness, is common in those who use these calamities to discover and claim their true identity. His father, a doctor, quit his practice and devoted himself full time to Julio's rehabilitation. During his convalescence, he learned to play the guitar and found that he loved to sing.

Chart 15

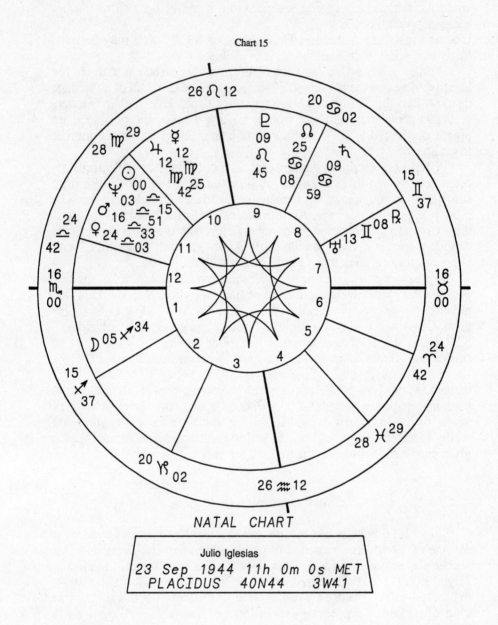

NATAL CHART

Julio Iglesias
23 Sep 1944 11h 0m 0s MET
PLACIDUS   40N44   3W41

Julio's chart is shown here as Chart 15. In the birth chart, Uranus makes squares to the tenth house Mercury and Jupiter and an opposition to the first house Moon. (A wide t-square) We will see these same aspects repeated in key transits and solar returns. This combination shows not only his charisma, but the possibility that an accident could have a strong, positive effect on his career choice. His father's helpfulness is shown by the tenth house Jupiter in the t-square.

The exact date of his accident is not known, but during July, 1963, Uranus traveled from 2 to 3 Virgo, in the tenth house (career). Pluto traveled from 9 to 10 Virgo, and the Midpoint would be from 5 to 6 Virgo, squaring his natal Moon, setting off the natal aspect. The solar return for 9/23/62, in effect at the time of the accident, is shown here as Chart 16. The opposition from Pluto and Uranus in the sixth to Jupiter in the twelfth, its most beneficial house position, show not only the accident, but the growth that came during his convalescence. The solar return for 9/24/63 at 0:22:39 in Madrid is not shown, but repeats the natal Moon in Sagittarius, this time square Uranus, as well as the natal Saturn/Neptune square.

One of the most famous stars of the Sixties generation also had one of the most famous accidents of that time. Bob Dylan was at the height of his popularity when he suffered a devastating motorcycle crash on 7/29/66. In the subsequent nine months of seclusion, there were rumors that he was actually dead or a vegetable or that he was hideously deformed. When he emerged, finally, his style was significantly changed to a more mellow and religious one. It seems likely that freedom-loving Dylan unconsciously had the accident to get away from the controlling effect of his fame. About the period just prior to the crash, he has said that the pressure was unbelievable and very painful.

Transits for his accident in Woodstock, NY on 7/29/66 are printed around the outside of the wheel, with noon used for the calculations, although the exact time is unknown.[2]

As befits a famous radical, Dylan's natal chart, shown here as Chart 17, has a prominent Uranus. It is part of a fifth house stellium, conjunct Saturn, the Moon, and Jupiter in Taurus as well as his Gemini Sun. Again, those with a prominent natal Uranus seem more prone to serious accidents, as they learn the lessons of self-will. By transit, Pluto and Uranus are conjunct and could conceivably be squaring his Sagittarius Ascendant, if the birth time were off slightly. They do semisextile the given Midheaven. Note that he had recently been undergoing a two-way Neptune/Saturn transit, with transiting Saturn opposite natal Neptune and transiting Neptune opposite natal Saturn. We would conclude that he was suffering some disillusionment with success and with the limits placed on his high ideals. The further conversation of his music to a more religious theme would also be suggested by this combination.

Chart 16

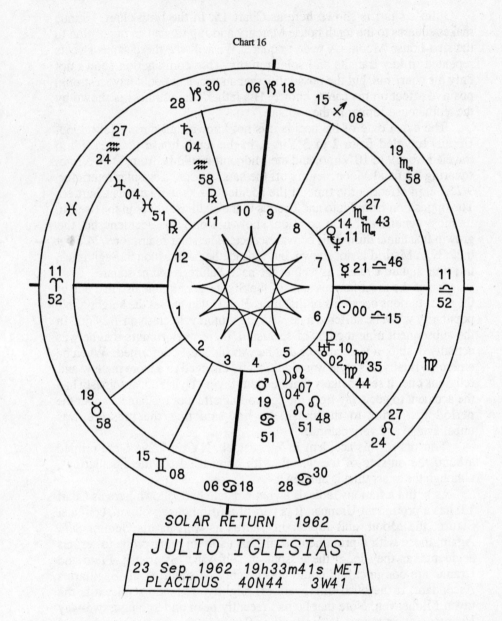

SOLAR RETURN 1962

JULIO IGLESIAS
23 Sep 1962 19h33m41s MET
PLACIDUS 40N44 3W41

Chart 17

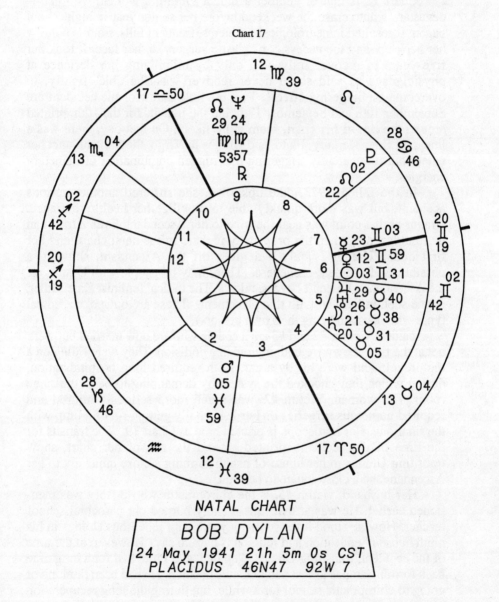

NATAL CHART

BOB DYLAN
24 May 1941 21h 5m 0s CST
PLACIDUS 46N47 92W 7

Chart 18 is that of another accident victim, a woman who had a devastating auto crash the weekend before her senior year in high school began. It resulted in neurological problems, frequent falls, trouble holding her neck up, and the necessity of plastic surgery on her face. It took her five years to recover fully, and only by mobilizing her defiance at physicians who said she'd never recover was she able, finally, to overcome the lingering effects. Two possible dates for the accident are September 10th and September 17th, but the transits for the 10th, printed around the rim of her chart, seem more likely. On that day, there was a lineup of Sun, Mercury, Pluto, and Uranus in Virgo, the Sun conjunct her natal Saturn apparently triggering this rugged combination of planetary· energies.

In the fall of 1973, date unknown, she suffered another serious accident, but was more quickly able to mobilize her healthy defiance. Uranus at that point was near the trine to her Ascendant. Even a trine can be troublesome, when the propensity is there in the natal chart, and her first house Uranus is only 9 degrees off the Ascendant, showing a possibility of accident-proneness. (There may be people with Uranus on the Ascendant who don't have accidents. The radical feminist Kate Millet, is one such individual with this placement. These are outspoken radical types who insist on being their own person.)

Accident victims #2 and #3 are a couple who are now married but were not at the time they were both injured in a collision. They were riding on a motorcycle and were hit by a car. Both required long hospitalization, during which they shocked the system by demanding to be in the same room. The woman, Victim #2, was much more seriously injured and required numerous surgeries on her leg, finally getting rid of a limp with the final one. Her horoscope is printed here as Chart 19. The transits for the time of the accident, printed around the rim of her chart, show transiting Uranus in her house of health forming a close quincunx to her Ascendant and a close square to her Sun.

Her husband, victim #3, is the chiropractor whose story was mentioned earlier. He was at that time a badly burned out parochial school teacher. How he stood it for so many years with rebellious Uranus in his ninth house of education and religion is hard to say. However, at the time of the accident, transiting Uranus, Neptune, and Pluto had for a long time been forming angles to that natal Uranus position. He had been thinking of going to chiropractic school for a while, but during the long recuperation period, he finally made a move forward. He is now a chiropractor who uses many advanced and New Age tools in his work. His chart is printed here as Chart 20.

As an additional point of interest, the composite chart between victims #2 and #3 is printed as Chart 21. The accident-prone Mars/Uranus square

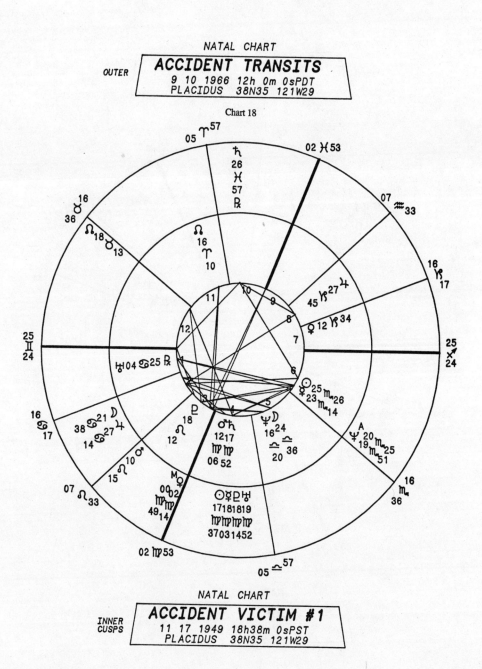

NATAL CHART

ACCIDENT TRANSITS

OUTER

9 10 1966 12h 0m 0sPDT
PLACIDUS 38N35 121W29

Chart 18

NATAL CHART

ACCIDENT VICTIM #1

INNER
CUSPS

11 17 1949 18h38m 0sPST
PLACIDUS 38N35 121W29

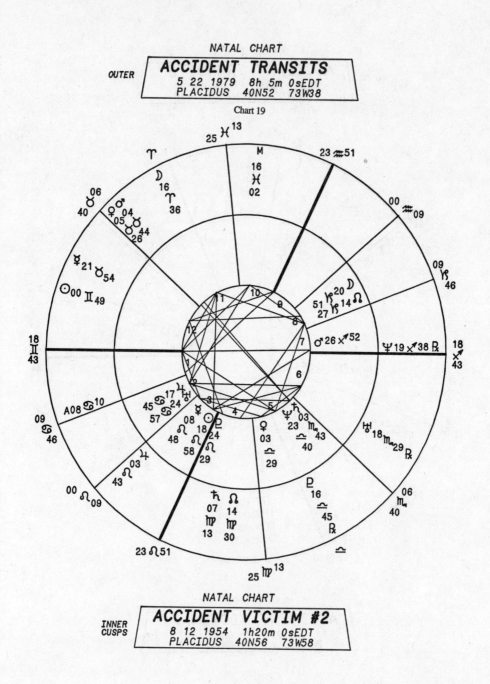

NATAL CHART

ACCIDENT TRANSITS
5 22 1979   8h 5m 0sEDT
PLACIDUS   40N52   73W38

OUTER

Chart 19

NATAL CHART

ACCIDENT VICTIM #2
8 12 1954   1h20m 0sEDT
PLACIDUS   40N56   73W58

INNER
CUSPS

is in the composite, as would fit two people jointly involved in a serious accident. Mars is in Libra (togetherness) and in the third house, which would rule short trips. The presence of Uranus-ruled Aquarius on the seventh house also hints that the accident itself had something to do with cementing the relationship. At the time of the crash, transiting Uranus was squaring the composite's first house Pluto, and appears to have broken down the reserve and barriers to closeness you would expect with such a position. It was also sextile the Venus of the composite.

Uranus rules adolescence, among other things, and Rick Nelson was a rock idol in his teens, never again to reclaim his popularity. In his birth chart, printed here as Chart 22, Uranus is conjunct his Sun and Midheaven, trining Neptune in the first.[3] His one real remaining moment of fame was an act of rebellion in refusing to stay locked into 1950s rock and roll songs at a reunion concert in Madison Square Garden. The adverse reaction of those who attended spurred his song Garden Party. The next we heard of him, he was dead in an airplane crash in Texas, with cocaine reputed to be the cause. The transits for that crash, on New Year's Eve, 1985, are printed around the rim of the chart and show a Uranus/Mercury conjunction a few degrees from a square to his Neptune and an opposition to his Mars. Perhaps more crucial here, since this is a death chart, are the Pluto aspects, which in two ways repeat a wide natal square between Saturn and Pluto. At the time of his death, transiting Pluto, along with Mars in Scorpio, was opposite his natal Saturn, while transiting Saturn was trine his natal Pluto.

It will be evident from studying this series of charts that transiting aspects are not always exact at the time of the accident, although they have generally been in effect for some time before it. No doubt it would take more precise and refined techniques like midpoints and planetary pictures to pinpoint an exact pattern. One traditional astrological teaching seems to hold true, however, which is that nothing happens by transit that is not already promised in the natal chart. Each of these individuals shows some propensity to accidents in the birth map.

Preventing Accidents

The purpose of this chapter is to help clients prevent serious injuries. A prediction which comes true is a feather in the astrologer's cap, while a non-event, such as an avoided accident, is impossible to prove, so I cannot say whether this method works. I would rather be helpful than right, so during the session I share the perspective outlined here when it appears a client might be in danger.

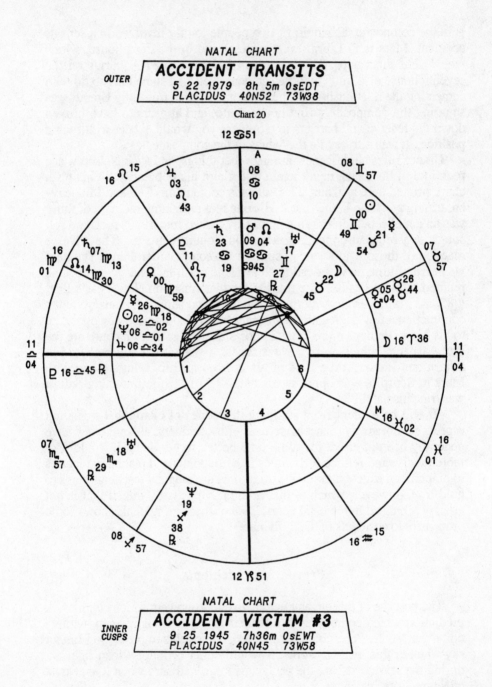

NATAL CHART

ACCIDENT TRANSITS

OUTER

5 22 1979   8h 5m 0sEDT
PLACIDUS   40N52   73W38

Chart 20

NATAL CHART

ACCIDENT VICTIM #3

INNER
CUSPS

9 25 1945   7h36m 0sEWT
PLACIDUS   40N45   73W58

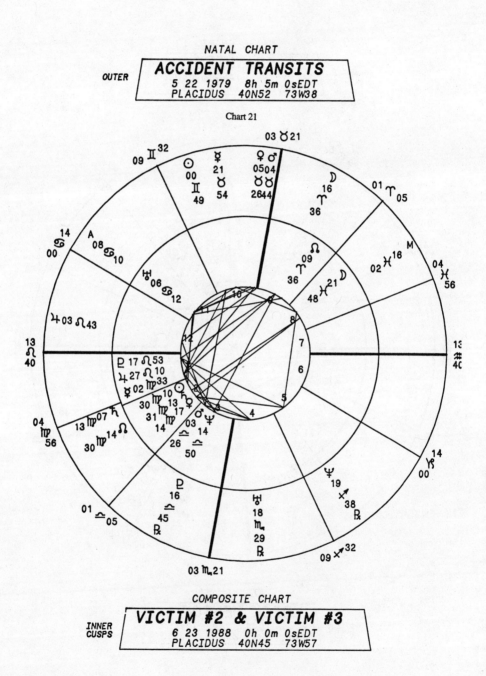

NATAL CHART

ACCIDENT TRANSITS
OUTER
5 22 1979   8h 5m 0sEDT
PLACIDUS   40N52   73W38

Chart 21

COMPOSITE CHART

VICTIM #2 & VICTIM #3
INNER
CUSPS
6 23 1988   0h 0m 0sEDT
PLACIDUS   40N45   73W57

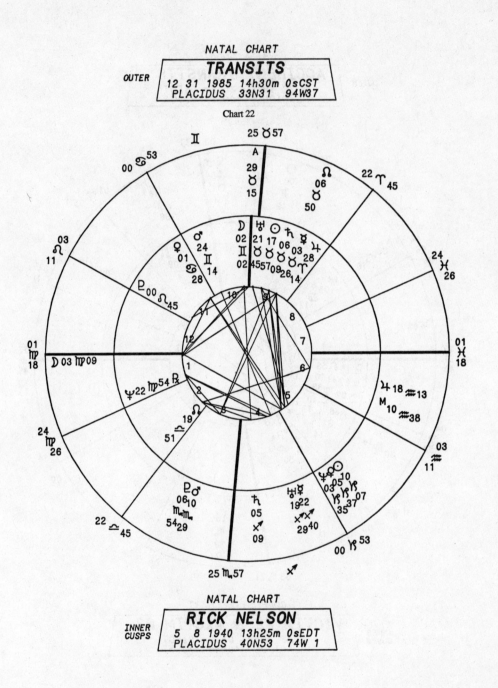

NATAL CHART
TRANSITS
OUTER
12 31 1985 14h30m 0sCST
PLACIDUS 33N31 94W37

Chart 22

NATAL CHART
RICK NELSON
INNER
CUSPS
5 8 1940 13h25m 0sEDT
PLACIDUS 40N53 74W 1

The ASTROLOGICAL signals, as stated in the beginning, could be Uranus transits to the Ascendant/Descendant axis, to the Midheaven, to Mars, to a first, sixth, or twelfth house planet, or while Uranus is transiting those houses and aspecting some important point. The PERSONAL or BEHAVIORAL signals would be that people experience a series of minor or near-accidents as the Uranus transit approaches. In addition, people are vulnerable due to severe stress related to some other Uranian event such as a separation or being fired. They may be frustrated, wanting change, and yet feeling stuck in a situation which no longer represents their true path. They may also be in a reckless or rebellious state of mind, no longer caring about consequences. REMEMBER THAT ACCIDENTS HAPPEN WHEN PEOPLE AREN'T BEING TRUE TO THEMSELVES.

In discussing divorce as one possible outcome of a Uranus transit, I advised against predicting divorce, since this is such a word of power that it could even turn the tide of events in that direction. You may wonder if the same holds true of accidents. YOU DEFINITELY SHOULD PREDICT—you won't suggest someone into an accident if the consultation is done properly. On the contrary, if an accident is a way of declaring independence and getting free, astrologers help people by exploring what areas they feel trapped in and supporting them in getting more freedom. The chart can help you be more specific about where that need for freedom lies. In these consultations, I may consciously make use of the strange spiritual authority my seemingly mysterious knowledge confers. Like it or not, it is there, and one might as well use it when it is possible to do so helpfully. I use this authority to give the client permission to be themselves.

For instance, if the aspects are forming in the sixth house, I explore how clients feel about their work. Generally, they say they cannot stand their jobs any longer and they'd like to go into free lance work, but feel unable because of responsibilities or fear of change. I discuss the possibility of an accident and explore whether any near-accidents have already occurred. (These might be on-the-job accidents. Serious accidents of this type entitle one to workman's compensation and vocational retraining, a possible underlying motive.)

We discuss why the need for more freedom and individual expression cannot safely be ignored, then explore how they could move toward free lance work or career change. We consider what schooling might be required, what leads to follow to build up business contacts gradually, and so on. The need for astrologers to have realistic, solid grounding in vocational matters is evident here. Other sixth house meanings—such as getting fired or a health crisis of a circulatory nature—are also discussed, relating back to the crucial issue of career change.

If the aspect were forming in the first house, I read this as a desire to change your persona to reflect your real self more accurately. People may have felt a lifelong constraint to conform to family or social pressures, so they act in a way alien to their true natures. During the transit, the wish builds up to rebel against social norms and shock others in a somewhat adolescent way. If they continue to conform, the resulting anger and frustration can erupt in an accident or in a health crisis. I explore the false facade and its effects on their most committed relationships (the Ascendant/Descendant connection). I give clients permission to allow their real selves to shine through.

I won't give interpretations of other accident aspects, for practicing astrologers can apply these ideas to individual charts. It would be important, however, given a Mars/Uranus transit, to devote considerable tim o exploring people's way of dealing with anger and to finding constructive mean. 'o express it. In service of prevention, astrologers could write down peak periods of danger, say when the aspect is most exact or when the Moon or Mars is making connections to transiting Uranus or the natal planet. You could also have people watch the phases of the Moon, since the data cited earlier shows they are most accident prone at the phase of the Moon they were born under and its opposite. (Teach them what those two phases look like in the sky.) You might also suggest they get their biorhythms done—or dig out the neglected free biorhythm program that came with your computer, marking critical and double critical days.

You may be wondering if concentrating on accidents frightens the client. My clients do not find it so, for we discuss the potential causes and look into ways to relieve the frustration that might bring one on. Given tools for prevention, the client is left with a sense of control. By this process, Uranus's expression can be upleveled from more difficult manifestations to more positive ones, such as the fuller development of consciousness and individuality.

Essences to Prevent or Heal Accidents

There are several remedies that can be helpful for accident victims. Immediately afterwards, take undiluted rescue remedy every two hours for several days, then continue in diluted form, along with SELF HEAL, which stimulates the body's capacity to heal itself. Over the long run, one component of RESCUE REMEDY, STAR OF BETHLEHEM, would be recommended, even for an accident that happened long in the past, for it releases old shock and trauma from the energy body. The herb comfrey is good for bones, and the flower essence COMFREY eases head injuries, nerve regeneration, and muscle aches. Essences and elixirs which would help the potential accident victim include PENNYROYAL, DAFFODIL, FORGET ME NOT, EMERALD, and AMETHYST. FORGET ME NOT enables one to respond more quickly to emergencies.

1 Dunbar Flanders, MD., *Your Preteenager's Mind and Body,* (NY: Hawthorn, 1962), p.48.
2 Lois Rodden, *Astro-Data II*, (San Diego, CA:ACS), 1980.
3 Michel and Francoise Gauquelin, *The Gauquelin Book of American Charts*, (San Diego, CA:ACS), 1982.

CHAPTER TEN

VIBRATIONAL HEALING AND ASTROLOGY

The Relationship of this Book to Several Others

This book is one of three books I have written dealing with the outer planets. I originally conceived of it as a single book entitled *The Outer Planets and Inner Life* but there was far too much material for it to fit into a single volume. The space requirements expanded along with my own consciousness of the outer planets. The first-published of the series, *Healing Pluto Problems* contains very specific remedies and exercises for working with problems related to the planet Pluto—family traumas, toxic secrets, guilt, resentment, and grief. This second book has concentrated on phenomena related to Saturn and Uranus—accidents, fear, depression, divorce, and the mid-life crisis, and has given suggestions for healing problems associated with them.

The third of the series will focus on Neptune phenomena—psychic development, schizophrenia, creativity, spirituality, and addiction—as well as some healing tools for getting to a more positive expression of Neptune. It will also consider a variety of topics related to the outer planets and to the work of the consulting astrologer. The same tools you have become familiar with in this book and the one on Pluto will continue to be used in this third volume. While you can gain helpful information from each of them, the three as a whole represent my personal perspectives on the outer planets. Thank you for joining me in the adventure of exploring the outer planets and discovering healing correlations for them.

Astrology and Vibrational Healing

This volume is called *Astrology and Vibrational Healing*. In closing, we should look at why that title was chosen. Vibration is a New Age buzzword, and yet there is a reason why it is used so often. On a subtle level, we perceive the reality of vibration. We sense the subtle shifts in vibratory levels between individuals and between the vibratory state of a given individual at different times of life.

The physical body, like all forms of matter, vibrates. Brain waves and electrocardiograms are but two means of measuring these energy pulsations and fluctuations. The subtle bodies, chakras, and various layers of the aura are even more subject to pulsations and fluctuations of the vibratory rate. Yet changes in these far more subtle forms of matter are vastly more difficult to measure. Astrology is a means of attuning to changes in vibratory state, both personal and collective. Each planet in our solar system and each of the twelve signs of the zodiac describes a particular type and focus of energy, a particular rate of vibration.

The study of the birth chart is a method for indentifying the interplay of subtle vibrations and energies in our lives. The vibration of Saturn is different from the vibration of Uranus, the vibration of Uranus is different from that of Neptune, and so on. Some of these vibrations are characteristic of the individual—certain people can be identified as primarily Saturnian, Plutonian, Venusian, or as typifying one or more of the other planets. Moreover, certain of these vibrations become important at different times in our lives—transient states, as accompanied by transits. Without astrology to provide a map, we don't recognize these unfolding energy patterns and how to channel them, we only know that we are depressed, fatigued, resentful, restless, or burned out.

Thus the study of astrology is an unsurpassed tool for identifying shifts of vibration and blockages of energy flow through the physical and subtle bodies, as well as the vibratory rate of the collective. If astrology works, it is not because of causation but of reverberation. That is, Saturn and Uranus do not cause the problems you meet, but they vibrate to the same frequency as the energies that are entering your life when you get a transit by those planets. They may very well be the lenses through which cosmic energies are focused.

Astrology can help by quickly identifying what is going on. A one-hour chart reading with a qualified astrologer shortcuts diagnosis—you may get a sharper, clearer picture of what is going on and more insight into where certain patterns come from than you do in meandering around for six months in the exploratory phase of traditional therapy. Of course, astrology cannot replace therapy when it is needed, but rightly used—not placing the blame for your problems onto the stars—it is a powerful tool for insight and for increasing consciousness. Consciousness, in itself, is a powerful healer, stripping away the blinders of denial and moving us out of the status of unconscious automatons. A chart reading can provide a Uranian jolt into a new level of consciousness. It can also be a preventative—helping you avoid unwise uses of energy or self-destructive applications of what is in essence a positive impulse.

How Astrology Combines
With Vibrational Healing Tools

Combined with certain tools, study of the birth chart can boost healing into a fine degree of specificity. In the chapter on homeopathic astrology, we talked about how like cures like—how picking a Saturn remedy for a Saturn problem makes healing more effective. Knowing which remedies are efficacious for a Saturn problem, and administering them at a time when Saturn is strong by transit, can enhance the healing. Thus, another contribution astrology can make to the art of healing is in pinpointing timing. Knowing which blockages are accessible to healing at a given time means that you are working with the flow of energy—and the deepest desire of the client—rather than against it.

The resonance between the planet, the healing tool, and the energy body of the individual is profound and worthy of further study. Homeopathic astrology—the theoretical underpinning of this book and the others in the series—seeks to indentify these resonances. Healing on the vibrational level is desirable, because it helps you retune or attune the subtle bodies, like tuning an instrument. When a problem manifests on the physical level, it has usually already existed on the subtle body level for some time—corresponding with the long slow approach of an outer planet in transit. If you start with the physical and stay with it, you are only responding to the symptoms, not striking at the cause, which is some form of imbalance. When the energies flow unhindered through the various bodies, from the causal to the physical, you're on the road to true health and well-being.

Light is the clearest instance of vibratory healing, in that color has to do with energy frequencies. The subtle form of light in the aura, as used in the various meditations and exercises in this book, penetrates and strengthens the energy body. Sound is obviously a form of vibration. The chants based on astrology are vibratory in nature, evoking and strengthening a specific part of the brain and energy body that corresponds to that planet. The level on which the flower remedies operate most strongly is also on the subtle bodies. Energy work, such as polarity therapy, Mariel, Reiki, or touch for health are also powerful.

To astrologers, I recommend the study of these vibrational tools. To healers, I recommend the study of astrology, a profoundly useful x-ray of the variety of levels on which any personal problem operates. We are just beginning to glimpse the potentials of vibrational healing and to understand the contribution astrology can make to it. Those of us who investigate these correspondences must also share them with others. In sharing them and getting feedback, we come to understand them on a deeper level, not remaining boxed in by our own personal limits and blind spots, but joining our personal experience to the experiences of other seekers. Such sharing can also save valuable time, for we do not have decades for this knowledge to evolve; we need to know it now, so as many people as possible can be helped in the shortest possible time.

Some Thoughts on Numerology and Vibrational Healing

Numerology is undoubtedly another science of vibration. I have never succeeded in getting as much information from numerology as from astrology, but that possibly is only because astrology is more closely related to my own cognitive process than are numbers. As I wrote this closing chapter, however, some very exciting possibilities for the use of numerology began to emerge.

It may be, for instance, that each crystal and each flower essence is attuned to a particular number, and that on a day, month, or year corresponding to particular numbers, you would benefit from the stone or remedy attuned to that number. Possibly the Latin names of the plants should be used, since each plant has different names in different languages. For instance, what Americans call Bleeding Heart is known in England as Love Lies Bleeding.

Individuals whose birthdates or names add up to given numbers would be most helped to overcome long-standing patterns by the corresponding healing tools. For instance, the word REBIRTHING consists of many nines and twos, and it is thought by some that two correlates with the Moon and nine with Neptune. Thus, rebirthing might be helpful for the people with the Moon and Neptune strong in their charts, especially in aspect to one another. Missing numbers might also be made up for by particular kinds of remedies. People who are missing a six, for instance, and thus have difficulty with relationships, might be helped by remedies vibrating to six which also have to do with relating.

This is a new idea to me, and an exciting one—perhaps a future direction. I intend to get a numerology program for my computer to add up all those remedy names. However, I cannot hope to reach an experienced numerologist's depth of understanding of what a missing six or an overemphasis of fives may mean. Such people can add much to the study of personal vibratory patterns. Numerologists who are drawn to healing could do us all a service by exploring these healing correlations and communicating their insights to us.

Astrology and the Healing of the Collective

Because the earth is but one body in the solar system, astrology, the mapping of planetary interaction, also helps us to key into what is going on with the Whole. The earth evolves, the solar system evolves, just as do individuals within it. As much as Wonderbread metaphysicians like to delude themselves that we have unlimited free choice in determining our lives, there is a limit to how far humanity can evolve unless we pay attention to the needs of the earth.

Individual healing is the focus of this book, and is a global cause *sine qua non*, and yet without collective healing, without global healing, the healing of individuals is continually undone. Our personal ills and dis-eases correspond, far more than we individualistic Americans would like to accept, with the ills of the collective—not just national, but global. Even less are we willing to accept that our health and growth are limited by the state of the earth, even though we are but interconnected cells in the body of that organism. Yet many now complain of depletion, not recognizing that what we feel, what we react to, and where this exhaustion originates, is in the depletion of the earth.

We are part of the earth, and we cannot escape feeling as she does. She is ill—we have made her ill through our exploitation and pollution of her resources—and we need to take care of her and ourselves in the years to come. Otherwise as the outer planets move into Aquarius and Pisces, there can be much suffering for mankind. The outer planets have moved out of the personal signs into the universal ones, and now the narcissistic ME generation must put personal concerns aside for the collective good. The flower and gem spirits have volunteered to help with this healing, giving us tools for boosting the vibrational level of mankind as a whole, but they cannot—and should not—do it for us.

We must consciously use the most positive potential of the current outer planet positions. We can use the healing and regenerative power of Pluto in Scorpio to halt and repair the damage. During this sojourn of the outer planets in Capricorn, we must come to accept the collective and personal responsibility for what is happening to us. We can use the planning and visionary foresight of Uranus and Neptune in Capricorn, the capacity to sacrifice for a worthwhile long-term goal, to give us the discipline and self-restraint to begin the process of rebuilding.